MINITAB

Student Version

Release 12

for Windows®

by

Minitab Inc.

Duxbury Press
An Imprint of Brooks/Cole Publishing Company
I(T)P® An International Thomson Publishing Company

Pacific Grove • Albany • Belmont • Bonn • Boston • Cincinnati • Detroit • Johannesburg • London
Madrid • Melbourne • Mexico City • New York • Paris • Singapore • Tokyo • Toronto • Washington

Duxbury Press is an imprint of Brooks/Cole Publishing Company
A Division of International Thomson Publishing Inc.
I(T)P The ITP logo is a registered trademark used herein under license.
Duxbury Press and the leaf logo are registered trademarks used herein under license.

For more information, contact Duxbury Press at Brooks/Cole Publishing Company:

BROOKS/COLE PUBLISHING COMPANY
511 Forest Lodge Road
Pacific Grove, CA 93950
USA

International Thomson Publishing Europe
Berkshire House 168–173
High Holborn
London WC1V 7AA
England

Thomas Nelson Australia
102 Dodds Street
South Melbourne, 3205
Victoria, Australia

Nelson Canada
1120 Birchmount Road
Scarborough, Ontario
Canada M1K 5G4

International Thomson Editores
Seneca 53
Col. Polanco
11560 México, D. F., México

International Thomson Publishing GmbH
Königswinterer Strasse 418
53227 Bonn
Germany

International Thomson Publishing Asia
60 Albert St.
#15-01 Albert Complex
Singapore 189969

International Thomson Publishing Japan
Hirakawacho Kyowa Building, 3F
2-2-1 Hirakawacho
Chiyoda-ku, Tokyo 102
Japan

Printed in Canada.

12   13   14

Table of Contents

Welcome to MINITAB Student Release 12

MINITAB Student Release 12 is a powerful statistical software package that provides a wide range of data analysis and graphics capabilities; intuitive user interface; clean, clear output; and extensive, context-sensitive on-line help. MINITAB Student offers the ideal combination of power, accuracy, and ease of use to help you do your work better.

At a glance, MINITAB Student Release 12 offers you the following:

- Comprehensive statistics capabilities, including basic statistics, regression, analysis of variance, sample size and power calculations, time series, cross-tabulations, and simulations and distributions.

- High-resolution graphics which are presentation-quality, fully editable and include a brushing capability for identifying points on plots and pinpointing the actual data point in the Data window. Paste graphs into other applications and edit them via OLE.

- Quality assurance and improvement features, including run charts, Pareto charts, cause-and-effect (fishbone) diagrams, and statistical process control charts

- Powerful data management capabilities. Import data from other versions of MINITAB, spreadsheets, databases, and text files into a project. Easily create subsets of your data.

- A graphical interface that provides an easy-to-use, efficient work environment.

How to Use *Meet MINITAB: Student Version*

This book is not designed to be read from cover to cover. It is designed to provide you with quick access to the information you need.

Whether you are a new or a prior MINITAB Student user, you should be sure to review the information in Chapter 1, *MINITAB Essentials*. There are some major new concepts in the use of MINITAB—saving projects, multiple worksheets—and this is an excellent introduction.

This book provides introductory and overview information to help you get "up and running" quickly, including several sample sessions.

Assumptions

This guide assumes that you know the basics of using Microsoft Windows 95/NT. This includes using menus, dialog boxes, a mouse, and moving and resizing windows. If you are not familiar with these operations, see your Microsoft Windows 95/NT documentation.

MINITAB on the Internet

Users all over the world can access MINITAB information 24 hours a day on the world wide web at http://www.minitab.com. With just a few keystrokes, visitors can access MINITAB macros and maintenance releases; comprehensive, up-to-the-minute information about the company and its products; press releases; product reviews; capabilities lists; newsletters; technical support information; the *Companion Text List*; and samples of MINITAB output. A search engine helps you find the information you need quickly. You can also provide feedback to the web site developers.

About the Documentation

To help you use MINITAB most effectively, Minitab Inc. and other publishers offer a variety of helpful texts and documents. The software itself provides on-line Help, a convenient, comprehensive, and useful source of information.

Documentation for MINITAB Student Release 12

MINITAB Help, 1998, Minitab Inc. This comprehensive, convenient source of information is available at the touch of a key or the click of the mouse. In addition to complete menu and dialog box documentation, you can find overviews, examples, guidance for setting up your data, information on calculations and methods, and a glossary. A separate help file is available for session commands.

Meet MINITAB: Student Version, 1998, Minitab Inc. Combining the brevity of our popular *MINITAB Mini-Manual* with our sample sessions creates this book. Rather than fully document all features, this book explains the fundamentals of using MINITAB— how to use the menus and dialog boxes, how to manage and manipulate data and files, how to produce graphs, and more. This guide includes four step-by-step sample sessions to help you learn MINITAB quickly.

For the first time, printed documentation—*Meet MINITAB: Student Version*—is included in Portable Document Format (PDF) files along with the Acrobat Reader for your use in using this publication electronically. You may view it on-line with the Reader, or print portions of particular interest to you.

Related Documentation

Companion Text List, 1996, Minitab Inc., State College, PA. More than 300 textbooks, textbook supplements, and other related teaching materials which include MINITAB are featured in the *Companion Text List*. For a complete bibliography, the *Companion Text List* is available on-line at http://www.minitab.com/ctl.htm.

MINITAB Handbook, Third Edition, 1994, Barbara F. Ryan, and Brian L. Joiner, Duxbury Press, Wadsworth Publishing Co., Belmont, CA. A supplementary text that teaches basic statistics using MINITAB. The Handbook features the creative use of plots, application of standard statistical methods to real data, in-depth exploration of data, simulation as a learning tool, screening data for errors, manipulating data, transformation of data, and performing multiple regressions. Please contact your bookstore, Minitab Inc., or Wadsworth Publishing Co. to order this book.

Typographical Conventions Used in this Book

C	denotes a column, such as C12 or 'Height'.
K	denotes a constant, such as 8.3 or K14.
M	denotes a matrix, such as M5.
Enter	denotes a key, such as the Enter key.
Alt + D	denotes pressing the second key while holding down the first key. For example, while holding down the Alt key, press the D key.
File ➤ Exit	denotes a menu command, such as choose Exit from the File menu. Here is another example: **Stat ➤ Tables ➤ Tally** means open the Stat menu, then open the Tables submenu, then choose Tally.
Click **OK**.	Bold text is also used to clarify dialog box items and buttons.

Sample Data Sets

For the examples in *Meet MINITAB: Student Version*, you can use data already stored in sample data set files in the DATA subdirectory of the main MINITAB directory.

MINITAB comes with a number of sample data sets, stored in the DATA and STUDENT subdirectories (folders). For complete descriptions of most of these data sets, see the Help topic *data set descriptions*.

Student Release 12 Capabilities Summary

General

- Menu interface, command-line option
- One CD-ROM runs on Windows NT or Windows 95
- Easy to use manual and HELP
- Documentation helps you analyze your data using MINITAB and interpret your results
- Session window: edit; paste output into word processor with formatting intact; save output in RTF format
- 32-bit processing for faster speed
- variable names can be up to 31 characters
- context-sensitive pop-up menus, and a Toolbar and status bar

Data and File Management

- Multiple worksheets
- Import/Export: Excel, Lotus 1-2-3, Quattro Pro, dBASE, and text files
- Preview any worksheet file before importing
- Import date and time data: use it in graphs, for subsetting, and for analyses
- Calculator
- Spreadsheet-like Data window for entering and editing data
- Insert and move columns in the Data window
- Specify the order in which you would like text categories processed by MINITAB commands
- Data manipulation: merge, stack, subset, sort, recode
- Create new worksheets easily with new, easy data subsetting
- Font control in Data window
- Store descriptive information with a project
- Save graphs, worksheets, and session output in one file
- Use numeric, text, and date/time data for categorical variables in analyses, such as ANOVA, and tables
- Double-precision worksheets

Basic Statistics

- Descriptive statistics, with both numerical and graphical summaries
- Store descriptive statistics easily
- Confidence intervals, one- and two-sample t-tests, paired t-tests
- Paired t-test and t-interval
- Estimation and tests for 1 and 2 proportion problems
- p-values for correlation

Regression Analysis

- Simple and multiple linear regression
- Model selection using stepwise or best subsets regression
- Plot the regression line with confidence and prediction bands
- Identification of unusual observations, model diagnostics, prediction/confidence intervals for new observations
- Residual plots
- Binary logistic regression and diagnostic plots
- Polynomial regression, with or without log transforms

Analysis of Variance

- Multiple factor ANOVA for balanced models, fixed and random effects
- Expected mean squares, approximate F tests
- Sequential and adjusted sums of squares, identification of unusual observations, model diagnostics
- Residual, main effects, and interaction plots
- Tests of homogeneity of variances

Tables

- Cross-tabulations
- Contingency tables
- Goodness-of-fit test

Statistical Process Control

- Run chart
- Pareto chart
- Fishbone diagram
- Control charts: XBar, XBar-R, XBar-S, R, S, I, MR, I-MR, MA, EWMA, p, np, c, u

Sample Size and Power Calculations

- 1-sample Z, t, and proportion
- 2-sample t and proportion
- One- and two-way ANOVA

Graphics

- Presentation-style graphics
- Scatter plots, box plots, histograms, charts, time series plots, matrix plots, draftsman plots
- Numerous special-purpose graphs
- Built-in graphs in analysis commands
- High-resolution dotplot
- Ability to customize all attributes of every element in your graph: color, type size, fonts, data display, and annotation
- Powerful, easy-to-use graph editor
- OLE: edit MINITAB graphs in other applications
- Graph brushing: displays values of user-selected points on plot, points are highlighted in all relevant graphs, and in Data window
- Subset and analyze data, based on brushed points
- Save graphs in TIFF, JPEG, PNG, and bitmap file formats

Time Series Analysis

- Autocorrelations, partial autocorrelations, and cross correlations
- Univariate Box-Jenkins ARIMA analysis: seasonal and nonseasonal with forecasts
- Trend analysis: linear, quadratic, exponential, or S-curve

- Decomposition: multiplicative or additive models
- Single or double exponential smoothing
- Winter's additive and multiplicative methods for exponential seasonal smoothing
- Moving average

Nonparametrics

- Sign test and confidence interval
- Wilcoxon test and confidence interval
- Mann-Whitney test and confidence interval
- Kruskal-Wallis test
- Friedman test for two-way layout
- Runs test
- Mood's median test
- Pairwise averages, differences, and slopes

Simulation and Distributions

- Random number generator: binomial, Poisson, normal, Weibull, beta, exponential, and logarithmic
- Density distribution, and inverse cumulative distribution functions
- Random sampling, with or without replacement

What's the Difference Between the Student and Professional Versions of *MINITAB*?

The Student Version of MINITAB is a streamlined and economical version of the professional software. It has most of the statistical methods and all of the ease-of-use features of the professional Release 12 software. But it has a smaller worksheet capacity and does not have some of the more advanced capabilities.

For a detailed list of the differences, open the Feature List Help file in the Minitab folder. (You can use the Windows Explorer to do this.) Click where indicated in the top paragraph of the opening screen.

If you would like to upgrade to the professional version of MINITAB, or just find out more about our products and services, please visit our web site: www.minitab.com

1

MINITAB Essentials

Before You Start

What you should know before you begin

This guide, as well as the Help files that came with the MINITAB software, assumes that you know the basics of using your computer—how to start applications, use your mouse, move and close windows, etc. If you need help doing these tasks, consult your system documentation.

What you will learn

MINITAB *Essentials* introduces you to the MINITAB environment and provides a quick overview of some of the most important features. For a step-by-step tutorial of some of this same information, see Chapter 8, *Session One: MINITAB Basics*.

If your screen looks different

MINITAB for Windows Release 12 can be used with Windows 95, Windows NT 4.0, and Windows NT 3.51. Depending on which version of Windows you are using, the pictures of dialog boxes, windows, and other software features you see in the documentation may not exactly match what you see on your screen.

Don't worry—the *contents* of the dialog boxes and windows, as well as the steps you follow to do something in MINITAB, are almost always the same no matter what version of Windows you use. Where there are exceptions, the documentation will point them out.

Starting and Exiting

▶ **To start in Windows 95 or Windows NT 4.0**

1   From the Taskbar, choose **Start ➤ Programs ➤ Minitab Student 12 ➤ Minitab**.

▶ **To start in Windows NT 3.51**

1   Locate and open the **Minitab Student 12** program group.

2   Double-click the **Minitab** icon ☰ .

▶ **To exit MINITAB**

1 Choose **File ➤ Exit**.

The MINITAB Environment

As you perform your data analysis, you will work with many different Minitab windows and tools. Here is a brief overview of the parts of the Minitab environment:

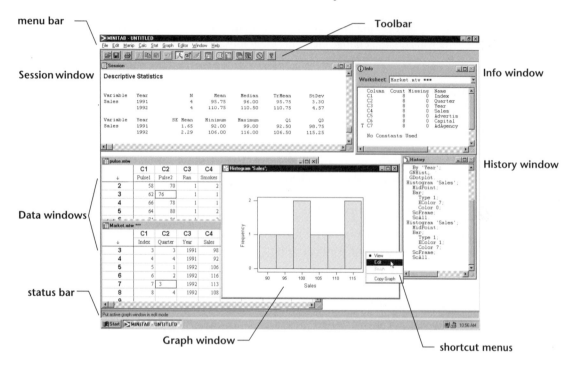

MINITAB windows

- The **Session window** displays text output such as tables of statistics.

- **Data windows** are where you enter, edit, and view the column data for each worksheet.

- The **Info window** summarizes each open worksheet. Choose which worksheet to view by picking from the drop-down list.

- The **History window** records all the commands you have used.

- **Graph windows** display graphs. You can have up to 15 Graph windows open at a time.

Menus and tools

- The **menu bar** is where you choose commands. See *Menu commands* on page 1-5.

- The **Toolbar** displays buttons for commonly used functions—the buttons change depending on which MINITAB window is active. See *The Toolbar* on page 1-5.

- The **status bar** displays explanatory text whenever you are pointing to a menu item or Toolbar button.

- **Shortcut menus** appear when you right-click on any window in MINITAB. The menu displays the most commonly-used functions for that window.

- Two graph editing palettes (not shown), the **Tool palette** and the **Attribute palette**, let you add and change elements on graphs. See *Graphing Data Overview* on page 5-2.

Work Flow in MINITAB

There are many steps you may take in a typical analysis. Each of the six chapters that follow this one correspond to a basic step in your analysis. Each chapter provides an overview of that step, and shows you how to perform some of the most common tasks for that part of your analysis.

The basic tasks and procedures that can be used throughout all the steps—such as issuing commands and working with projects—are described later in this chapter.

Here is a list of the chapters and a brief description of some of the tasks you will learn:

Chapter and title	Shows you how to...
2 *Managing Data*	enter and edit data in a Data window, add data from files and save to files, and generate patterned data
3 *Manipulating and Calculating Data*	manipulate columns of data in the Data window, sort and subset data, and create equations
4 *Using Data Analysis and Quality Tools*	use a variety of analysis procedures, from basic statistics to quality control
5 *Graphing Data*	create, edit, and brush graphs, as well as print and save graphs in a variety of formats
6 *Managing the Session Window and Generating Reports*	navigate through text output and change the format of text, as well as print and save output in a variety of formats
7 *Session Commands and Execs*	use command language interactively or within an Exec. Execs are useful for automating repetitive tasks.

Issuing Commands

In MINITAB, there are three ways to access commands: with menus, the Toolbar, and session commands.

Most commands use data in some way: they draw graphs based on the data, change existing data, or create data. Data are stored in worksheets, and a project can contain many worksheets. When you issue a command (by any method) that uses data, the command acts on the *current worksheet*. The current worksheet is the one associated with the *active Data window*. You make a window active by clicking on it or choosing it from the Window menu. If no Data window is active, the command acts on the Data window that was most recently active.

Tip | You can tell which Data window contains the current worksheet by looking at the window's title bar. The current worksheet will have three asterisks in the title, like this:

Menu commands

- **Menu bar**: Click on an item in the menu bar to open the menu, then click on a menu item to execute the command, open a submenu, or open a dialog box.

- **Shortcut menu**: Right-click in a MINITAB window to open the shortcut menu, then click on a menu item as in regular menus.

If a menu item is dimmed, it is currently unavailable.

Tip | To recall the last dialog box you used in your current MINITAB session, choose **Edit ➤ Edit Last Dialog** or press Ctrl+E.

When you open most dialog boxes, MINITAB "remembers" all of its settings from the last time you used the dialog box in this session. To clear a dialog box of all of its settings and return it to the default state, press F3.

The Toolbar

The Toolbar is a quick way to issue commands. When you click a button, MINITAB performs an action or opens a dialog box, exactly like the corresponding menu command.

The Toolbar buttons change depending on which MINITAB window is active. For example, here is the Toolbar when the Data window is active.

The Data window Toolbar

| Tip | To see the name of the button, place your mouse pointer over the button.
 To hide the Toolbar, choose **Window ➤ Hide Toolbar**. |

| More | When you edit graphs, two floating graph palettes also display. For details, see Chapter 5, *Graphing Data*. |

Entering variables in a dialog box

MINITAB's dialog boxes are like most of the ones you have used in other software. One feature that may be new to you is MINITAB's variable list box, which appears in many dialog boxes. The variable list box displays columns or stored constants, and lets you enter them into any text box that can accept variables. Of course, you can always type the variable name in the text box, but using the variables list box is usually faster and more error-free.

The variable list box contains columns and constants from the current worksheet.

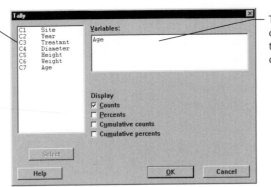

The **Variables** text box can accept only columns. When the cursor is in this box, the variable list box (left) displays only columns.

When you click on or place your cursor in a text box that can accept a variable, the variable list box displays all the variables in the current worksheet that are valid choices. For example, if the text box can accept only columns (but not stored constants), the variable list box will display only columns. If the text box can accept only numeric columns (but not text or date/time columns), the variable list box will display only numeric columns.

| Note | If the variable list box doesn't display the variables you expected, make sure that the worksheet you want is current: click **Cancel** to leave the dialog box, click on the Data window that belongs to the worksheet you want, then press Ctrl+E to return to the dialog box. |

▶ To select multiple variables with the mouse

1 Click in the text box you want to fill.

2 Click in the variable list box.

3 Click on individual variables, drag across several variables, or hold down Ctrl and click on discontiguous variables.

4 Click **Select.**

▶ **To select a single variable with the mouse (quick method)**

1 Click in the text box you want to fill.

2 Move your mouse pointer to the variable list box and double-click on the variable you want.

▶ **To select a variable using the keyboard**

1 Tab to the text box you want to fill.

2 Press F2 . This makes the variable list box active.

3 Using the up- and down-arrow keys, move to variable you want.

4 Press F2 . This makes the text box active again.

Session commands

Session commands are a useful alternative to menu commands, especially when making Execs to automate repetitive analyses. Most session commands are simple, easy to remember words, like PLOT, SAVE, or SORT. You can type commands in two places: the Command Line Editor and the Session window. Most often you will find it easier to use the Command Line Editor.

▶ **To use the Command Line Editor**

1 Choose **Edit ➤ Command Line Editor.**

Paste, type, and edit commands here.

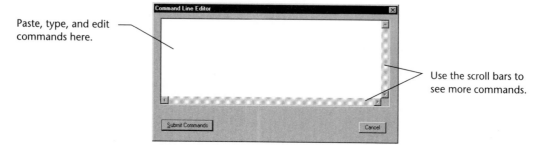

Use the scroll bars to see more commands.

2 Do one of the following:

- Type the session commands—see *Basic Rules for Typing Session Commands* on page 7-3.

- Paste them from the History window by pressing Ctrl + V .

3 Click **Submit Commands.**

Working with Projects

A MINITAB project contains all your work: the data, text output from commands, graphs, and more. When you save the project, you save all of your work at once. When you open a project, you can pick up right where you left off. You can have only one project open at a time.

The project's many pieces can be handled individually. You can create data, graphs, and output from within MINITAB. You can also add data and graphs to the project by copying them from files. The contents of most windows can be saved and printed separately from the project, in a variety of file formats. You can also *discard* a worksheet or graph, which removes the item from the project without saving it. See *Working with Individual Windows* on page 1-9.

Opening, saving, and closing projects

When you save the project, you save all the information about your work:

- the contents of all the windows, including
  - the columns of data in each Data window
  - the stored constants that are summarized in the Info window
  - the complete text in the Session and History windows
  - each Graph window

- the description of each project created with **File ➤ Project Description**

- the description of each worksheet created with **Editor ➤ Worksheet Description**

- the size, location, and state of each window

- the contents of each dialog box you used

▶ To open, save, or close a project

- To open a new project, choose **File ➤ New**, click **Project**, and click **OK**.

- To open a saved project, choose **File ➤ Open Project**.

- To save a project, choose **File ➤ Save Project**.

- To close a project, you must open a new project, open a saved project, or exit MINITAB.

Note | If you close a project before saving it, MINITAB will prompt you to save the project. You choose to save the entire project in a project file, or save pieces of the project in separate files. For details on separate files, see *Saving the contents of each window* on page 1-11.

Saving project preferences

When you save a project, you not only save the contents of windows and dialog boxes, you also save their size, location, and appearance. If you want to use these same settings when you start a new project, you can save your preferences.

▶ **To save your preferences**

1 Choose **Edit ▶ Preferences**.

2 Click the category of preferences you want to save, such as **Data window**, then click **Select**.

3 Change the settings you want, click **OK**, then click **Save**.
   The next time you start a new project, MINITAB will use these settings.

Working with Individual Windows

Projects are made up of data, text output, graphs, and information about the current working environment. Most of this information is visible in one of MINITAB's windows; for example, the text output is visible in the Session window. Data in MINITAB is slightly unusual in that the contents are visible in more than one window—see *Understanding data and worksheets* below.

Much of the content of various windows is created within MINITAB. For example, the Session window contains the output of analysis commands, the History window holds all the commands you have used, and the Data window can contain data that you have typed in directly.

Worksheet data and graphs, however, can also come from outside files—see *Adding worksheets and graphs from files* on page 1-10. Worksheets and graphs can also be *discarded*, that is removed, from the project—see *Closing worksheets and graphs* on page 1-11. The Session, History, and Info windows cannot be discarded.

The contents of all of the windows can be saved into a separate file and printed.

Note | The number of Data windows you can have open at one time is limited to five. Once this number is exceeded, an error message will appear, and you will have to close one or more open data sheets before continuing.

You can have up to 100 Graph windows open at one time.

Understanding data and worksheets

Each data set you work with in a project is contained in a *worksheet*. You can have up to five worksheets in one project. Each worksheet can contain up to 5000 cells.

View and edit a worksheet's contents through MINITAB windows and commands:

- View your data in MINITAB's Data, Info, and Session windows

- Edit columns of data in a Data window (one Data window for each worksheet)

- Manipulate and analyze data using commands

When you issue a command that effects your data, the command acts on the current worksheet. For details, see *Issuing Commands* on page 1-5.

Adding worksheets and graphs from files

You can add worksheets and graphs to the project by copying from data and graph files. Worksheet data can be from MINITAB worksheet (MTW) files, or from other applications, like Excel. Graph window content can come only from MINITAB Graphics Format (MGF) files.

Worksheet and graph files work differently than in earlier releases of MINITAB. When you open a file, you are *copying* the contents of the file to the project. That means that any changes you make to the worksheet or graph inside the project will not affect the file itself. If you do want the changes to be reflected in that file, you can save the worksheet or graph with that same name, overwriting the old file's contents.

▶ To add worksheet data or graphs from a file

1   Choose **File ▸ Open Worksheet** or **File ▸ Open Graph**.

This opens a standard Windows file dialog box. For help on using the dialog box, click the **Help** button.

2   Select a directory and file name.

If you are opening a worksheet, by default the dialog box displays the file names of all MINITAB worksheet (MTW) files. If you want to copy data from a file that is not a worksheet (for example, a MINITAB project (MPJ) file or an Excel file), select that file type from the **Files of type** drop-down list.

3   Click **Open**.

A message box will appear, telling you that a copy of the content of this file will be added to the worksheet. If you do not want this message to appear every time you open a file, check **Do not display this message again**.

4   Click **OK**.

More | For more information on opening worksheet files, see *Opening, Saving, and Printing Files* on page 2-9.

Closing worksheets and graphs

When you no longer need the worksheet or graph in your project, you can close it. Closing removes the item from the project, and the data or graphs are gone forever.

You can close a worksheet or graph by clicking the close button on the Data or Graph window's title bar (just as you would close any window on your system), or you can use the menus as described below.

▶ To close a worksheet

1   Make the desired Data window active.

2   Choose **File ➤ Close worksheet**.

3   MINITAB will ask if you want to save the worksheet first. Click **Yes**, **No**, or **Cancel**, as you prefer.

▶ To close graphs

1   Choose **Window ➤ Manage Graphs**.

2   Under **Graphs**, click on the name of one or more graphs.

3   Click **Close**, then click **Done**.

More | You can close all graphs at once by choosing **Window ➤ Close All Graphs** or clicking the button.

Saving the contents of each window

You can also individually save and print the contents of any window. This is handy if you want to share one particular data set with a colleague, export a certain graph so it can be used in another MINITAB session, or use the Session window text in a word processor.

▶ To save the contents of a window

1   Activate the window you want to save.

2   Choose **File ➤ Save [window type] As**.

3   Pick a file type—see the table below.

4   Enter a file name and click **OK**.

Available file types

You can save your data and results in various file types, depending on what you want to save.

Save these contents	as these file types	File extension
Session window output	■ Plain text—no fonts ■ Rich Text Format—fonts ■ List files—same as plain text	■ TXT ■ RTF ■ LIS
Worksheet data that will work in MINITAB Release 12: columns, constants, and all other worksheet features	■ Release 12 worksheet	■ MTW
Worksheet data that will work in an earlier release of MINITAB: columns, constants, and worksheet features specific to that release	■ Release 11 worksheet ■ Release 10 worksheet	■ MTW ■ MTW
Worksheet data that will work in any release of MINITAB: columns and constants	■ Portable worksheet	■ MTP
Columns only	■ Excel ■ Lotus 1-2-3 ■ and more	■ XLS ■ WK1
Graphs	■ MINITAB Graphics Format (graphs that can be re-opened in MINITAB) ■ Graphics formats that can be used in other applications, such as bitmap format	■ MGF ■ BMP ■ TIF ■ JPG ■ PNG
History window contents	■ Plain text with a variety of file extensions. For example, MTB files are MINITAB Execs.	■ TXT ■ MTB ■ and more
Info window contents	■ Plain text	■ TXT

Printing the contents of windows

▶ To print a window

1 Make the window active.

2 Choose **File ➤ Print [Window Name]**.

3 If you are printing a Data window, MINITAB will display an options dialog box. Select the options you want, and click **OK**.

4 In the Print dialog box, click **OK**.

Tip | To print a portion of the window, first select the text or cells you want, follow steps 1–3 as above, then in the Print dialog box make sure **Print Range** is set to **Selection**.

Getting Answers and Information

This book is designed to give you an overview of the most important features of MINITAB, but sooner or later you will want more details. You have several resources for finding answers.

Resource	Description	How to get it
Readme file	Late-breaking information on this release of MINITAB, including details on changes to the software or documentation	From the Windows taskbar, choose **Start ➤ Programs ➤ Minitab Student 12 ➤ Readme file**. In Windows NT 3.51, double-click the Readme icon.
On-line Help	Complete documentation on each MINITAB feature and concept, written for users of menus and dialog boxes, and organized especially for on-line viewing	In MINITAB, you can ■ choose **Help ➤ Contents** ■ click the **Help** button in any dialog box ■ press F1 at any time ■ click 🔘 on the Toolbar
Session Command Help	Documentation on each session command, including syntax and examples	From the Start menu, choose **Programs ➤ Minitab Student 12 ➤ Session Command Help**. In Windows NT 3.51, double-click the Session Command Help icon.
Feature List	A Help file containing a concise listing of all MINITAB Student 12 features and a comparision of the Student Version with the professional version of Release 12	From the Start menu, choose **Programs ➤ Minitab Student 12 ➤ Feature List**. In Windows NT 3.51, double-click the Feature List icon.

Resource	Description	How to get it
Internet	At Minitab Inc.'s web site you can get answers to common technical questions, download Execs, and download free maintenance releases of MINITAB	Go to *HTTP://www.minitab.com* and follow the support links.

Where to Go Next

Now that you have an idea of how to use MINITAB to analyze your data, what is the best way to proceed?

If you would like more practice with MINITAB, turn to the *Sample Sessions* which begin with Chapter 8, *Session One: MINITAB Basics*. These are step-by-step tutorials that guide you through sample analyses.

Or just jump in and begin your own analysis, referring to on-line Help or the printed documentation whenever you have a question.

2
Managing Data

Managing Data Overview

In this chapter, you will see the many ways for you to bring data into MINITAB. You can type data, copy and paste it, or generate it from within MINITAB, and of course, open it from files.

When you are finished working with the data, you can save it to use later in MINITAB or another application. Or you can print a hard copy.

But first, you should become familiar with some of the terminology and concepts used when managing your data in MINITAB.

Data are contained in worksheets

In MINITAB, all the data associated with a particular data set are contained in a *worksheet*. A project can have up to five worksheets, each containing up to five thousand cells.

A worksheet can contain three types of data—numeric, text, and date/time—in two forms: columns or constants. You can view your data in several windows, but most of the time you will work with columns of data in the Data window.

Three types of data: numeric, text, and date/time

- *Numeric* data are numbers.

- *Text* data are characters that can consist of a mix of letters, numbers, spaces, and special characters, such as "Test Number 4" or "North Carolina."

- *Date/time* data can be dates (such as Jan-1-1997 or 3/17/97), times (such as 08:25:22 AM), or both (such as 3/17/97 08:25:22 AM). MINITAB internally stores dates and times as numbers, but displays them in whatever format you choose.

Data can take two forms: column or stored constant

Form	Contains...	Referred to by Number	Name	Number available
Column	numeric, text, or date/time data	C + a number, as in C1 or C22	'Sales' or 'Year'	Limited only by system memory
Stored Constant	a single number or a text string (e.g., "New York")	K + a number, as in K1 or K93	'First' or 'Counter'	1000

Columns and constants are both:

- affected by menu and session commands

- named with the session command NAME (documented in Help)—though columns can also be named in the Data window

- saved to a file when you choose **File ➤ Save Current Worksheet (As)** or **File ➤ Save Project (As)**

- summarized in the Info window

Three windows to work with data

The Data window

This window contains the columns of data that are in the worksheet. When you have multiple worksheets open, each worksheet has its own Data window.

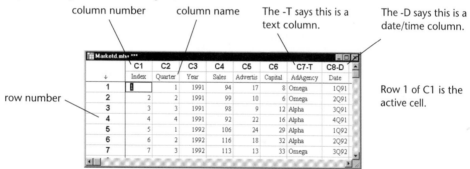

In each Data window you can

- view the columns of data that are in the worksheet

- enter values and edit them in various ways (see the following pages)

- manipulate columns in various ways, including changing the format, font, name, width, description, and position of columns (described in Chapter 3, *Manipulating and Calculating Data*)

Note | Data windows are not spreadsheets.

Although the Data window has rows and columns, it is not a spreadsheet like Microsoft Excel or Lotus 1-2-3. In MINITAB, cells contain values that you type or generate with commands. Cells do not contain formulas that update based on other cells.

For example, if you want column C3 to equal the values in C1 plus the values in C2, you would use the calculator to generate the values for C3 (see *Using the Calculator* on page 3-12). If you change the values in C1, C3 does not change until you use the calculator again or use some other command to change C3's contents.

The Info window

This window summarizes all the data in the active worksheet: columns and constants. You can also choose to see the information for any worksheet in the project. However, you cannot edit data in the Info window.

Text columns are noted with T.
Date/Time columns are noted with D.

All other columns are numeric.

Constants have their own section of the Info window.

To see the information on another worksheet, pick the worksheet name from the drop-down list.

The Session window

You can display columns and constants in this window when you choose **Manip ➤ Display Data**.

"Mean Sales" is a constant.

"Sales" is a column.

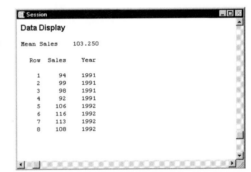

Typing Data into the Data Window

To enter a value in a Data window cell, just click on the cell, type a value, and press
Enter. You can enter multiple values in any order you wish: column by column, row by
row, or in blocks.

Each column of cells generally
represents a variable.

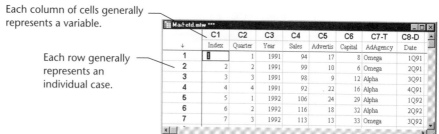

Each row generally
represents an
individual case.

Entering data automatically formats the column. When you type an entry into an
empty column, MINITAB assigns a data type to the column: numeric, text, or date/time.
If the data type is not numeric, MINITAB also adds an identifier next to the column
number: D for date/time data and T for text data.

More | You can change data from one type to another. See *Changing column data types* on page
3-6.

▶ **To open a new (empty) Data window**

1 Choose **File ➤ New**.

2 Select **Minitab Worksheet** and click **OK**.

Entering data in columns, rows, or blocks

▶ **To enter data columnwise**

1 Click the data direction arrow to make it point down.

2 Enter your data, pressing Tab or Enter to move the active cell. Press Ctrl+Enter to
move the active cell to the top of the next column.

data direction arrow

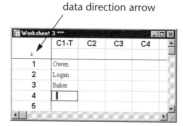

For example, click in row 1, column 1, then type:
   Owen Enter
   Logan Enter
   Baker Enter
Notice that after you type a value and press Enter,
the active cell moves down.

▶ To enter data rowwise

1 Click the data direction arrow to make it point to the right.

2 Enter your data. Press [Ctrl]+[Enter] to move the active cell to the beginning of the next row.

data direction arrow

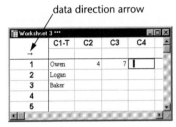

For example, click in row 1, column 2, then type:
4 [Enter] 7 [Enter]

Notice that after you type a value and press [Enter], the active cell moves right.

▶ To enter data within a block

1 Highlight the area you want to work in.

2 Enter your data. The active cell moves only within the selected area.

3 To unselect the area, press an arrow key or click anywhere in the Data window.

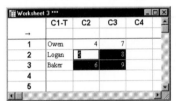

For example:
- With the mouse, point to the cell at row 2, column 2.
- Drag down and to the right. This selects the block.
- Type:
    5 [Enter] 8 [Enter]
    6 [Enter] 9 [Enter]

Notice that if you select a block before typing values, pressing [Enter] moves the active cell to the next cell in the block. Pressing any arrow key unhighlights the block.

If you make a mistake

▶ To correct a value in a cell

- To delete the old value and enter a new one, click the cell, type the correct value, and press [Enter].

- To change a portion of the cell contents, double-click the cell, then use the arrow, [Backspace] and [Del] keys to make the changes.

▶ To undo a change

- If you have just typed a new value in a cell, and have not yet pressed [Enter], press [Esc] to restore the previous value of the cell.

Copying and Pasting Data

Copying and pasting is a quick way to enter data that is in another application or in another MINITAB window. You can copy from

- cells in the same Data window, or from cells in another Data window

- another spreadsheet package, such as Lotus 1-2-3 or Microsoft Excel

- a table in a word processor or text in the body of a word processing document

- the MINITAB Session window

▶ **To copy from anywhere and paste into the Data window**

1 Highlight the data you want and copy it. In MINITAB, the copy command is **Edit ➤ Copy**.

2 In one of MINITAB's Data windows, select one or more cells, then choose **Edit ➤ Paste Cells**.

3 If you selected more than one cell, MINITAB will replace the contents of those cells with the contents from the Clipboard.

   If you selected one cell, MINITAB will ask how you want to paste data. Do one of the following and click **OK**:

   - Choose **Insert above the active cell, shifting cells down to make room**.

   - Choose **Replace the active cell**.

4 One of the following happens, depending on whether the data on the Clipboard is separated (or delimited) by tabs or spaces. Data copied from MINITAB's Data window, most spreadsheet packages, and word processor tables are tab-delimited. Data copied from MINITAB's Session window and the body of word processing documents are space-delimited.

   - If the data are separated by tabs, MINITAB automatically puts each value into its own cell.

   - If the data are separated by spaces, MINITAB displays a dialog box that shows the first line of data and asks how MINITAB should interpret the spaces. Do one of the following:
     – If the line of data looks right, click **Use spaces as delimiters**.
     – If you would prefer to paste all the data into one column, click **Paste as a single column**.

Tip | To undo, choose **Edit ➤ Undo Paste**.

Generating Patterned Data

You can generate data that follow a pattern. You can generate a simple set of numbers that follows a sequence, or a list of numbers that have an arbitrary order. You can also generate patterned date/time data.

The most common task is to fill a column with a simple set of numbers that follow a sequence: for example, all the numbers from 1 to 100, or all the even numbers between 1 to 50. Optionally, each value in the list can be repeated, or the entire sequence can be repeated. Repeating values or entire sequences can be very useful for entering factor levels for analysis of variance designs.

More | You can also generate random data—see Help for details.

▶ To generate a simple set of numbers

1 Choose **Calc ➤ Make Patterned Data ➤ Simple Set of Numbers**.

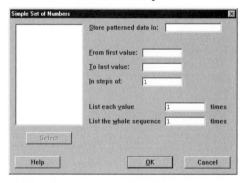

2 In the text box for **Store patterned data in**, enter the name or number of a new or existing column where you want the patterned data to go.

3 Enter numbers in the **From first value**, **To last value**, and **In steps of** text boxes.

4 Optionally, enter a number in **List each value** and/or **List the whole sequence**.

▷ **Examples of patterned data expressions**

To get...	From first value	To last value	In steps of	List each value	List the whole sequence
all the numbers from 1 to 100	1	100	1	1	1
all even numbers from 10 to 1: 10 8 6 4 2	10	1	2	1	1
every tenth between -0.5 and -0.1: -0.5 -0.4 -0.3 -0.2 -0.1	-0.5	-0.1	0.1	1	1
five 1's, five 2's, five 3's, and five 4's: 11111222223333344444	1	4	1	5	1
two sets of the sequence 12345, repeating each number: 11223344551122334455	1	5	1	2	2

Opening, Saving, and Printing Files

You can add data to your project by copying it from a file. The contents of each file are stored in a worksheet.

When you open a project file, all the worksheets that were inside that project when you last saved are available to you. When you save a project, the data are saved with that project.

Most of the time, the data files you will bring into your project will be MINITAB worksheets. Those worksheets may be stand-alone files (files with the extension MTW), or parts of a project (MPJ) file. You can preview a project file to see a list of all the worksheets in the file, then copy one of the worksheets from that project to your own.

You can also open and save data files from many other applications like Excel and Lotus 1-2-3, or exchange data with versions of MINITAB on other platforms using MINITAB portable worksheets (MTP files).

Opening data files

▶ To open data from a file

1 Choose File ➤ Open Worksheet.

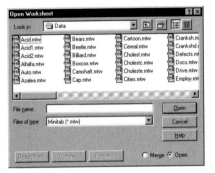

The appearance of this dialog box may be different on your computer, depending on which operating system you are using. For details, see your system documentation.

2 In the **Files of type** box, choose the type of file you are looking for: Excel, Lotus 1-2-3, MINITAB portable worksheet, etc.

3 Select a file.

4 If you like, use any of the options below, then click **Open**.

Options

■ When you select a MINITAB worksheet file, click **Description** to read the worksheet description, or click **Preview** to see the data before you open it. When you are *merging* a MINITAB file (see below), the Preview dialog box also lets you select which columns you want to merge and where to place them.

■ When you select a MINITAB project file, click **Preview** to see which worksheets are contained in the file. In that Preview dialog box, you can also view descriptions for each worksheet.

■ When you select a non-MINITAB file, click **Preview** to see how MINITAB will interpret the rows and columns. If you like, change column settings in the Preview dialog box, or click **Options** to change other settings.

■ For any file type, you can choose to **Open** or **Merge** the file. Opening creates a new worksheet that contains the data. Merging adds the data to the current worksheet.

Saving data

▶ To save data as part of the project

1 Choose File ➤ Save Project.

▶ To save data into a separate file

1 Make the desired Data window active.

2 Choose **File ➤ Save Worksheet As**.

3 In **Files of type**, choose the data format in which you want the data to be saved.

4 Select a directory, enter a file name, and click **OK**.

Printing data

▶ To print the contents of the Data window

1 Make the desired Data window active.

2 Choose **File ➤ Print Worksheet**.

3 Select or unselect options (at right), then click **OK**.

4 The standard Windows Print dialog box will appear. If you need instructions for using this dialog box, click the dialog box's **Help** button.

▶ To print all data, including constants

1 Choose **Manip ➤ Display Data**.

2 In the text box for **Columns and constants to display**, enter the variables and click **OK**. The data will appear in the Session window.

3 In the Session window, select the text.

4 Choose **File ➤ Print Session Window**.

5 Make sure **Print Range** is set to **Selection**, and click **OK**.

Working with Database and Special Text Files

This chapter has touched on only the most common ways to get your data into MINITAB. You can also use MINITAB's ability to read text files in a format that you specify. Most data-using applications on most platforms can generate a text file. If MINITAB does not correctly interpret rows and columns when you use the **File ➤ Open Worksheet** command, you can use **File ➤ Other Files ➤ Import Special Text** to specify a custom format. For instructions, see Help.

3

Manipulating and Calculating Data

Manipulating and Calculating Data Overview

Once you have data in a MINITAB project, you may need to rearrange or reorganize the data before you begin your analyses. You can move or delete rows and columns, convert data from one type to another (such as changing numeric data to date/time data), or control the way data is displayed in Data windows and graphs (such as displaying a date as 1/1/97 or January 1, 1997).

You can also create new variables that are based on the original variables. You can combine columns, create subsets of columns, or fill a column with values that are calculated from values in other columns.

Manipulating Cells, Rows, and Columns

You can perform a variety of actions on cells, rows, and columns in the Data window.

Before performing an action, you often select the area you want to affect. If you do not select a row or column before doing an operation that affects the entire row or column (such as insert column), the column that contains the active cell is considered selected.

Selecting areas of the Data window

▶ To select...	Do this
a block of cells	drag across the cells.
one or more entire rows	drag across the row numbers.
one or more entire columns	drag across the column numbers.
all the cells	choose **Edit ▶ Select All Cells**.

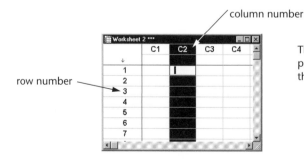

column number

row number

The active cell is always part of the selection—in this case, row 1 of C2.

Cutting, clearing, and deleting

Before cutting, clearing, or deleting, select an area or click on the cell you want to make active.

▶ **To delete...**

To delete...	Do this
cells and put them on the Clipboard (following rows or columns move up or left)	Choose **Edit ➤ Cut Cells**.
cell contents only (empty cells remain)	Choose **Edit ➤ Clear Cells**, or press [Backspace]. In a numeric column, MINITAB inserts * in a cleared cell (unless it is the last cell in a column).
cells (following rows or columns move up or left)	Choose **Edit ➤ Delete Cells** or press [Delete].

Copying and pasting

Before copying or pasting, select an area or click on the cell you want to make active.

▶ **To copy...**

To copy...	Do this
cells to the Clipboard	Choose **Edit ➤ Copy Cells**.
certain rows of columns This command copies columns from one part of a Data window to another part of a Data window, using or omitting rows you specify.	1 Choose **Manip ➤ Copy Columns**. 2 Click **Use rows** or **Omit rows**. 3 Enter criteria and click **OK**.

▶ **To paste cells from the Clipboard and...**

To paste cells from the Clipboard and...	Do this
replace other cells	1 Select the same number of cells that are on the Clipboard. 2 Choose **Edit ➤ Paste Cells**.
insert above a cell	1 Click on a cell. 2 Choose **Edit ➤ Paste Cells**. 3 A dialog box apears. Choose **Insert above the active cell** and click **OK**.

Note | If you paste from another MINITAB window, such as the Session window, or from another application, MINITAB may prompt you for instructions on how to paste the data. See *Copying and Pasting Data* on page 2-7.

Inserting emtpy cells, rows, and columns

▶ To insert cells, rows, or columns

1 Select one or more cells.

2 Choose **Editor ➤ Insert Cells/Insert Rows/Insert Columns**.

Cells and rows are inserted above the selection, columns are inserted to the left of the selection.

MINITAB inserts the same number of items that are selected. For example, if cells in three rows are selected when you choose **Editor ➤ Insert Rows**, three rows are inserted.

Moving columns

▶ To move columns

1 Select one or more columns.

2 Choose **Editor ➤ Move Columns**.

3 Select one of the following and click **OK**.

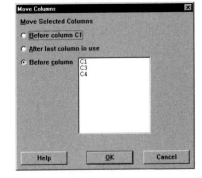

- **Before column C1** inserts the selected columns before C1 (pushing other columns to the right).

- **After last column in use** places the selected columns after the last non-empty column.

- **Before column** inserts the selected columns before whatever column you click in the list box.

Naming, sizing, and hiding columns

▶ To name a column

1 Click a column name cell.

2 Type the name. Names cannot:

- be longer than 31 characters

- begin or end with a space

- include the symbol ' or #

- start with or consist entirely of the symbol *

3 Press Enter.

▶ **To change the width of one or more columns**

1 Select the column(s).

2 With your mouse, point to the top of a line dividing a selected column from another column. The cursor becomes a two-sided arrow ◄|►.

3 Drag the border until the columns are the desired width.

▶ **To change the widths of all columns**

1 Choose **Editor ➤ Set Column ➤ Widths.**

2 In **Set column widths to**, enter a number. Click **OK.**

▶ **To hide and display columns**

If your data are spread out over the worksheet with many blank intervening columns— for example, a worksheet with data only in columns C1, C10, and C20—you may want to *compress* the Data window display. Compressing the display hides all the unused columns to the left of the last non-empty column; you will still see empty columns to the right of the last used column. Uncompressing returns the display to normal.

- To compress the display, choose **Editor ➤ Compress Display**. If you open the **Editor** menu again, you will see that a check mark now appears before **Compress Display.**

- To uncompress the display, choose **Editor ➤ Compress Display** again.

Changing Column Data Types and Formats

There are three *types* of data: numeric, text, and date/time. A column can contain only one type of data. You can assign a data type to an empty column and change the data type of existing columns of data.

Once a column has a data type, you can specify format characteristics for that column. When you modify the format characteristics of a column, you are only changing the way that column is displayed in the Data window and graphs—you are not modifying the underlying value.

For example, say that a cell contains the number 1.2345678. If you change the format to display only two decimals, the Data window cell will display 1.23, the label for that data point on a graph will display 1.23, but all calculations will still use 1.2345678. The Session window output for analysis commands will display the format used by that command, regardless of the Data window format.

You can also create descriptions for columns, and select the fonts you want to use to display labels and data in the Data window.

Changing column data types

▶ To apply a data type to an empty column

1 Choose **Editor ➤ Format Column**.

2 Choose **Numeric, Text,** or **Date/Time**.

▶ To change the data type of a non-empty column

1 Choose **Manip ➤ Change Data Type**.

2 Choose the conversion type you want.

3 Complete the dialog box and click **OK**.

Changing numeric and date/time formats

▶ To change the number of decimals displayed in a numeric column

1 Select one or more columns. The columns must be empty (unformatted) or already in numeric format.

2 Choose **Editor ➤ Format Column ➤ Numeric**.

3 Select **Fixed decimal width**. In the **decimal places** text box, type the number of decimals, and click **OK**.

▶ To change the way the date and time are displayed in a date/time column

A single date/time value can be a date, a time, or both. For example, all of the following are valid date/time values:

1/1/96
3:04 PM
1/1/96 3:04 PM

1 Select one or more columns. The columns must be empty (unformatted) or already in a date/time format.

2 Choose **Editor ➤ Format Column ➤ Date/Time**.

3 From the **Date/Time Column Format** box, select a format and click **OK**.

More | If you do not see a format you like in the Date/Time Column Format list, you can create your own in the **New format** text box. See Help for details.

Setting column descriptions and Data window fonts

▶ To create or edit a column description

Descriptions are useful for recording the source of the column's data, or for recording how the data have been modified from the source.

1 Choose **Editor ➤ Set Column ➤ Description**.

2 Type or paste the information you want, then click **OK**.

▶ To change Data window fonts

You can set the font for labels (column numbers, like C1, and row numbers), and one font for data (the column names and values in the cells).

1 Choose **Editor ➤ Select Fonts ➤ Select Label Font** or **Select Data Font**.

2 Set font properties, then click **OK**.

Subsetting and Splitting Data

Often you will want to perform analyses or create graphs for a group of observations within a larger data set. For example, you may want to focus only on the females in the study, or only on the sales revenue for a certain quarter. MINITAB can create a worksheet that contains only the subset you want; when you make that worksheet active, subsequent analyses or graphs will reflect only that subset.

You can subset a worksheet based on conditions, or split a worksheet based on all the groups in a specified variable.

Subsetting based on conditions

You can subset your data based on one or more conditions. For example, you could create a subset based on two conditions: quarterly sales revenues that are greater than 100 (in thousands of dollars) *and* quarterly advertising expenses that are less than 15 (also in thousands). The rows of data that meet both those conditions are copied into a new worksheet. The original worksheet will remain.

Original worksheet			**Subset in a new worksheet**		
Quarter	Sales	Advertis	Quarter	Sales	Advertis
1	94	17	3	113	13
2	99	10	4	108	14
3	98	9			
4	92	22			
1	106	24			
2	116	18			
3	113	13			
4	108	14			

▶ To subset based on conditions

1 Choose **Manip** ▶ **Subset Worksheet**.

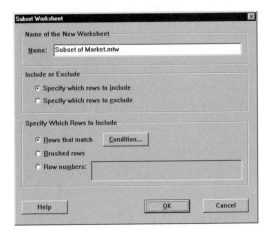

MINITAB automatically supplies a default name for the new worksheet, but you can change it if you like.

2 Under **Specify Which Rows to Include/Exclude**, choose **Rows that match** and click **Condition**.

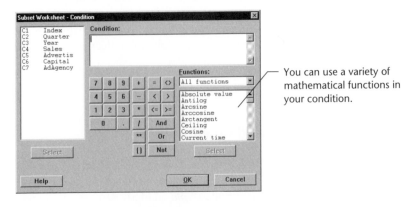

You can use a variety of mathematical functions in your condition.

3 In **Condition**, enter an equation which describes the condition. For example, to create a subset that contains only sales revenue higher than 100, you would enter: Sales > 100

Note that if you chose in the Subset main dialog box to *exclude* rows, this equation would create a subset that would contain all the sales values that were *not* greater than 100.

4 Click **OK** twice.

Splitting a worksheet by groups in a variable

You can *split* a worksheet into groups based on all the unique values in a variable. For example, say that you have a worksheet of sales data with two columns: the column Sales contains the total dollars in revenue for a fiscal quarter, and the column Quarter contains the quarter in which the sales figure occurred (1, 2, 3, or 4).

If you split the worksheet based on the variable Quarter, MINITAB will create four new worksheets: one in which all values in Quarter equal 1, one in which all the values in Quarter equal 2, and so on. The original worksheet will remain.

▶ To split a worksheet by groups in a variable

1 Choose **Manip** ➤ **Split Worksheet**.

2 In **By variables**, enter the column that contains the desired group. Click **OK**.

Stacking Columns

Sometimes you may need to combine two variables so you can analyze them with one command. MINITAB lets you easily stack the contents of columns on top of each other. You can store the stacked contents in another column, preserving the original columns.

When you stack columns, you can also create a column of subscripts, or identifier codes, that indicate which column an observation came from. Identifier codes can be used later to subset your data, to create graphs in which data points are displayed differently depending on which group they are from, or to unstack the columns.

For example, the Stacked column below contains the contents of Pulse1 stacked on the contents of Pulse2. We know that the value 88 comes from the second column (Pulse2) because the subscript is 2.

Pulse1	Pulse2	Stacked	Subscripts
64	88	64	1
58	70	58	1
62	76	62	1
66	78	66	1
64	80	64	1
		88	2
		70	2
		76	2
		78	2
		80	2

▶ **To stack columns**

1 Choose **Manip ➤ Stack/Unstack ➤ Stack Columns**.

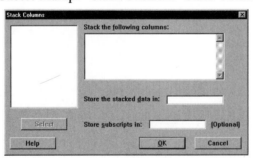

2 In **Stack the following columns**, enter all the columns in the order you want them stacked.

The first column you enter will be stacked on top of the second column, which will be stacked on top of the third column, etc. For example, entering *Pulse1 Pulse2* will stack the values in Pulse1 on the values in Pulse2.

3 In **Store the stacked data in**, enter a new or existing column.

4 Optionally, in **Store subscripts in**, enter a new or existing column where you want subscripts stored.

More | You can split a column into two columns using the command **Manip ➤ Stack/Unstack ➤ Unstack One Column**. For details, see Help.

Recoding Data

You can convert a value to another value, or convert a range of values to another value. You can recode numeric values to other numeric values (for example, converting all values from 1.0 to 1.9 to the value 1), text to text, text to numeric, or numeric to text.

For example, you could convert the data in the variable Sex from 1's and 2's to the words "Male" and "Female." The text values could be stored in a column named Gender.

```
Sex     Gender
 1      Male
 2      Female
 2      Female
 1      Male
```

▶ To recode numeric data to text data

1 Choose **Manip ➤ Code ➤ Numeric to Text**.

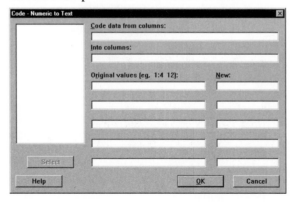

2 In **Code data from columns**, enter one or more columns, such as the column Sex.

3 In **Into columns**, enter one or more new or existing columns.

For example, if there is not a column named Gender, typing "Gender" would create a new column with that name.

4 In the first box under **Original values**, type a numeric value (for example, *1*) or range of values (for example, *1:12*, which means from 1 to 12).

5   In the first box under **New**, type the text value that the numeric value should be converted to. For example, to correspond to a value of 1 in the column Sex, you would type the word "Male." Do not include quotation marks.

6   Optionally, specify up to four other recodings in the remaining boxes, with a **New** value for every **Original** value.

Using the Calculator

The calculator lets you quickly perform basic arithmetic or complex mathematical functions. The results of the calculation can be stored in a column or constant.

▶ To use the calculator

1   Choose **Calc ➤ Calculator**.

2   In **Store result in variable**, enter a new or existing column or constant.

3   In **Expression**, select variables and functions from their respective lists, and click calculator buttons for numbers and arithmetic functions. You can also type the expression.

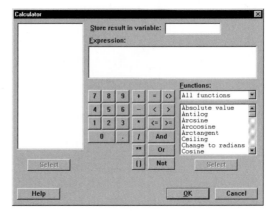

4   Click **OK**.

▷ Example of creating a column based on a calculation

In a study about pulse rates, you have two columns which contain the pulse rates of participants: Pulse1 and Pulse2. You can create a new column which is the difference between those two columns.

1   Open the file PULSE.MTW.

2   Choose **Calc ➤ Calculator**.

3   In **Store result in variable**, type *PulseDif*.

4   In **Expression**, enter the equation *Pulse2 - Pulse1*. You can type the equation, or click on variables in the list box and buttons on the calculator.

5   Click **OK**.

Data	Pulse2	Pulse1	PulseDif
window	88	64	24
output	70	58	12
	76	62	14
	78	66	12
	...	...	...

Interpreting the results

In the Data window, MINITAB creates the new column PulseDif, then stores the results there. The subtraction is done row by row.

More

MINITAB offers another way to manipulate and calculate data. For details on Random Data and Probability Distributions, see Help.

Random Data and Probability Distributions

You can generate random data with many different distributions, which is useful for simulations: choose **Calc ➤ Random Data** and pick a distribution name from the menu. You can also calculate probability densities, the cumulative probabilities, or the inverse cumulative probabilities of your data for a variety of distributions: choose **Calc ➤ Probability Distributions** and pick a distribution name from the menu.

4

Using Data Analysis and Quality Tools

Data Analysis and Quality Tools Overview

MINITAB provides many statistical and graphical techniques to analyze data. Available methods include:

- basic statistics
- regression
- analysis of variance
- control charts

- time series
- tables
- nonparametric analysis
- quality tools

For a complete list of capabilities, see *Student Release 12 Capabilities Summary* on page x. In addition, there is an overview topic in Help for each of the categories shown above. From there, you can move through the Help file to obtain information for a specific capability.

This chapter provides a sample of MINITAB's analysis capabilities including:

- basic statistics—descriptive statistics, one-sample t, and correlation
- regression—least squares regression
- analysis of variance—one-way ANOVA
- tables—cross tabulation
- control charts—$\overline{X}$ and R chart

More | MINITAB also provides many ways to graphically analyze your data. For more information, see Chapter 5, *Graphing Data* in this book.

Descriptive Statistics

MINITAB provides two commands, Display Descriptive Statistics and Store Descriptive Statistics, which calculate or store various statistics for each column or for subsets within a column. You can display these statistics in the Session window and optionally in a graph.

▶ To display descriptive statistics

1 Choose **Stat ➤ Basic Statistics ➤ Display Descriptive Statistics**.

2 In **Variables**, enter the column(s) containing the data you want to describe.

3 If you like, use one or more of the options listed below, then click **OK**.

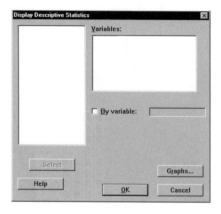

Options

- display separate statistics for each unique value in a "By" column—see the example below

- generate a histogram, a histogram with a normal curve, a dotplot, or a boxplot of the data in separate Graph windows, or display statistics in a single graphical summary

☞ Example of displaying descriptive statistics

You want to examine the weight (in pounds) of male (Sex = 1) and female (Sex = 2) students who participated in a pulse study.

1 Open the file PULSE.MTW.

2 Choose **Stat ➤ Basic Statistics ➤ Display Descriptive Statistics**.

3 In **Variables**, enter *Weight*.

4 Check **By variable** and enter *Sex* in the text box. Click **OK**.

Session window output

Descriptive Statistics

Variable	Sex	N	Mean	Median	Tr Mean	StDev	SE Mean
Weight	1	57	158.26	155.00	157.61	18.64	2.47
	2	35	123.80	122.00	123.74	13.37	2.26

Variable	Sex	Min	Max	Q1	Q3
Weight	1	123.00	215.00	145.00	170.00
	2	95.00	150.00	115.00	131.00

Interpreting the results

MINITAB displays descriptive statistics for the variable Weight in the Session window. Because you used the "By variable" Sex, there is one description for males (Sex = 1) and one description for females (Sex = 2). Not surprisingly, the results show that males (mean = 158.26) weigh more than females (mean = 123.80).

Confidence Intervals and Tests of the Mean

MINITAB provides commands for calculating confidence intervals and performing tests of the mean for one or two samples. Capabilities include a Z-test, one-sample t-test, two-sample t-test, and paired t-test.

MINITAB also provides methods for the evaluation of proportions and differences in proportions. In addition, MINITAB provides methods to calculate confidence intervals and perform hypothesis tests for the median when you cannot assume that your data is normally distributed.

A one-sample t-confidence interval and hypothesis test for the mean (assumed to be normally distributed) is shown below.

▶ **To compute a t-confidence interval and test of the mean**

1 Choose **Stat ➤ Basic Statistics ➤ 1-Sample t**.

2 In **Variables**, enter the column(s) containing the samples. MINITAB performs a separate analysis on the data in each column.

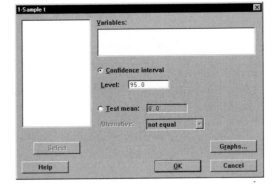

3 Do one of the following:

- to calculate a confidence interval for the mean, choose **Confidence interval**

- to perform a hypothesis test, choose **Test mean**

4 If you like, use one or more of the options listed below, then click **OK**.

Options

- specify a confidence level for the confidence interval. The default is 95%.

- specify a null hypothesis test value. The default is $\mu = 0$.

- define the alternative hypothesis by choosing less than (lower-tailed), not equal (two-tailed), or greater than (upper-tailed). The default is a two-tailed test.

- display a histogram, dotplot, and boxplot for each column

▷ Example of a t-confidence interval

Say that you want to obtain a 95% t-confidence interval for the mean resting pulse of a sample population.

1 Open the file PULSE.MTW.

2 Choose **Stat ➤ Basic Statistics ➤ 1-Sample t**.

3 In **Variables**, enter *Pulse1*. Click **OK**.

Session window output

Confidence Intervals

Variable	N	Mean	StDev	SE Mean	95.0 % CI
Pulse1	92	72.87	11.01	1.15	(70.59, 75.15)

Interpreting the results

Based on this output, you estimate the mean resting pulse to be 72.87, and you can be 95% confident that the true value falls between the upper and lower limits of the reported confidence interval (70.59 and 75.15).

Correlation

Use Correlation to calculate the Pearson product moment coefficient of correlation (also called the correlation coefficient or correlation) for pairs of variables. The correlation coefficient is a measure of the degree of linear relationship between two variables. The correlation coefficient assumes a value between −1 and +1. If one variable tends to increase as the other decreases, the correlation coefficient is negative. Conversely, if the two variables tend to increase or decrease together, the correlation coefficient is positive.

▶ **To correlate pairs of columns**

1 Choose **Stat ➤ Basic Statistics ➤ Correlation**.

2 In **Variables**, enter the columns containing the measurement data. If you enter more than two columns, MINITAB calculates the correlation between every pair of columns and prints the lower triangle of the resulting correlation matrix.

3 If you like, use either of the options listed below, then click **OK**.

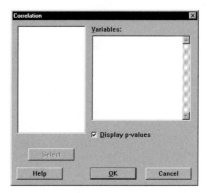

Options

- display the p-value for individual hypothesis tests. This display option is the default.

▶ **Example of a correlation**

Say you want to examine the relationship between the heights of students and their weights.

1 Open the file PULSE.MTW.

2 Choose **Stat ➤ Basic Statistics ➤ Correlation**.

3 In **Variables**, enter *Height* and *Weight*. Click **OK**.

Session window output

Correlations (Pearson)

```
Correlation of Height and Weight = 0.785, P-Value = 0.000
```

Interpreting the results

The correlation value (r = 0.785; p = 0.000) suggests that height and weight are positively correlated. Further tests could explore the significance of this correlation and give you a better idea of the relationship between height and weight. For example, this correlation and the following regression examples use the combined male and female data. It may be better to subset the data by sex to determine if the relationship between height and weight differs for males and females.

More | To calculate Spearman's ρ (rank correlation coefficient), rank the data in both columns using **Manip ➤ Rank** and then use **Correlation** on the ranked data.

By using a combination of MINITAB commands, you can also compute a partial correlation coefficient, which is the correlation coefficient between two variables while adjusting for the effects of other variables.

Regression

Regression analysis is used to investigate and model the relationship between a response variable and one or more predictors. MINITAB provides various least squares and logistic regression procedures. Least squares procedures include simple, multiple, stepwise, and best subsets regression. You can plot a fitted regression line and generate residual plots. MINITAB also provides a binary logistic regression method.

An example of the simplest form of regression, using the least squares method to fit a linear model, is shown on the following page.

▶ To do a linear regression

1 Choose **Stat ➤ Regression ➤ Regression**.

2 In **Response**, enter the column containing the response (Y) variable.

3 In **Predictors**, enter the columns containing the predictor (X) variables.

4 If you like, use one or more of the options listed below, then click **OK**:

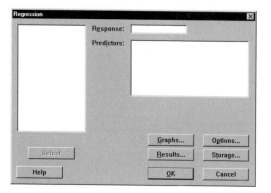

Options

- draw five different residual plots

- perform a weighted regression

- exclude the intercept (constant) term from the regression by unchecking **Fit Intercept**

- display the variance inflation factor (VIF) and Durbin-Watson statistic

- perform lack of fit tests

- predict the response for new observations

- store various statistics for model evaluation or further analysis

- control the display of results

▷ **Example of performing a simple linear regression**

Say you want to explore the relationship between weight and height.

1 Open the file PULSE.MTW.

2 Choose **Stat ➤ Regression ➤ Regression**.

3 In **Response**, enter *Weight*. In **Predictors**, enter *Height*. Click **OK**.

Session window output

Regression Analysis

```
The regression equation is
Weight = - 205 + 5.09 Height

Predictor        Coef        StDev          T        P
Constant      -204.74        29.16      -7.02    0.000
Height         5.0918       0.4237      12.02    0.000

S = 14.79      R-Sq = 61.6%      R-Sq(adj) = 61.2%

Analysis of Variance

Source            DF          SS          MS          F        P
Regression         1       31592       31592     144.38    0.000
Residual Error    90       19692         219
Total             91       51284

Unusual Observations

Obs    Height    Weight      Fit    StDev Fit    Residual    St Resid
  9      72.0    195.00   161.87        2.08       33.13        2.26R
 25      61.0    140.00   105.86        3.62       34.14        2.38R
 40      72.0    215.00   161.87        2.08       53.13        3.63R
 84      68.0    110.00   141.50        1.57      -31.50       -2.14R

R denotes an observation with a large standardized residual
```

Interpreting the results

The p-value of 0.000 suggests that weight is a significant predictor of height, and the R^2 value of 61.6% tells you the amount of variability in the response that this model accounts for.

More │ To work through an example of using regression, see Chapter 9, *Session Two: Doing a Simple Analysis*.

Analysis of Variance (ANOVA)

Analysis of variance (ANOVA) extends the two-sample t-test, which compares two population means, to a test that compares more than two means.

MINITAB's ANOVA capabilities include procedures for fitting one-way, two-way, and more complicated ANOVA models, a test of equal variances, and graphical procedures for viewing your data and understanding the fit of a model.

A one-way ANOVA tests for the equality of population means when classification is by single variable. Below, we show how to analyze data when the response data is in one column and there is a second column of level values identifying the population (*stacked* case). If you have data from each population in separate columns of your worksheet (*unstacked* case), you would use the One-way (Unstacked) command.

▶ To do a one-way ANOVA

1 Choose **Stat ➤ ANOVA ➤ One-way**.

2 In **Response**, enter the column containing the response.

3 In **Factor**, enter the column containing the factor levels.

4 If you like, use one or more of the options described below, then click **OK**.

Options

- store residuals and fitted values (the means for each level)

- display confidence intervals for the differences between means, using four different multiple comparison methods: Fisher's LSD, Tukey's, Dunnett's, and Hsu's MCB (multiple comparisons with the best)

- draw boxplots, dotplots, and five different residual plots

> ## Example of a one-way ANOVA

1 Open the file PULSE.MTW.

2 Choose **Stat ➤ ANOVA ➤ One-way**.

3 In **Response**, enter *Weight*. In **Factor**, enter *Sex*.

4 Click **Graphs**.

5 Check **Boxplots of data** and **Normal plot of residuals**. Click **OK** twice.

Session window output

Oneway Analysis of Variance

Analysis of Variance on Weight

```
Source    DF        SS        MS         F         p
Sex        1     25755     25755     90.80     0.000
Error     90     25529       284
Total     91     51284
                                  Individual 95% CIs For Mean
                                  Based on Pooled StDev
Level      N      Mean     StDev  --+---------+---------+---------+----
    1     57    158.26     18.64                            (--*-)
    2     35    123.80     13.37  (---*--)
                                  --+---------+---------+---------+----
Pooled StDev =     16.84          120       135       150       165
```

Graph window output

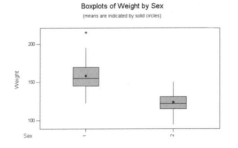

Boxplots of Weight by Sex
(means are indicated by solid circles)

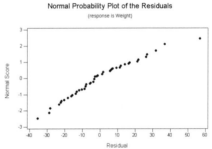

Normal Probability Plot of the Residuals
(response is Weight)

Interpreting the results

The analysis of variance output and boxplots clearly show that male and female weights are different. The high F-statistic and low p-value indicate there is a statistically significant difference between males and females. The 95% confidence interval for average weight of females is between about 118 and 130 pounds. For males, it is between about 155 and 162 pounds.

More | To work through an example of analysis of variance, see Chapter 10, *Session Three: Advanced MINITAB*.

Tables

Use MINITAB's table procedures to summarize data into table form or to perform a further analysis of this tabled summary. You can calculate various statistics or perform a χ^2 test for the tabled data. You can also perform simple or multiple correspondence analysis.

Cross Tabulation (shown below) displays one-way, two-way, and multi-way tables containing counts, percents, and summary statistics, such as means, standard deviations, and maximums, for associated variables.

▶ **To create a table of statistics**

1 Choose **Stat ➤ Tables ➤ Cross Tabulation**.

2 Do one of the following:

- For raw data, enter two to ten columns containing the raw data in **Classification variables**.

- For frequency or collapsed data:

    1 In **Classification variables**, enter two to ten columns containing the category data.

    2 Check **Frequencies are in** and enter the column containing the frequencies.

3 If you like, use one or more of the options listed below, then click **OK**.

Options

- display the counts and the row, column, and total percents of each cell within a two-way table

- perform a χ^2 test for association for each two-way table

- display the following for associated variables:
    - the mean, median, minimum, maximum, sum, and standard deviation for associated variables
    - the data, the number of nonmissing data, and the number of missing data
    - the proportion of observations equal to a specified value, and the proportion of observations between specified values for associated variables

- display the marginals for selected variables

- change the table layout

▷ Example of a two-way table displaying column percents

Suppose you want to summarize the data to obtain the number and percentage of smokers at each activity level.

1 Open the file PULSE.MTW.

2 Choose **Stat ➤ Tables ➤ Cross Tabulation**.

3 In **Classification variables**, enter *Smokes* and *Activity*.

4 Check **Column percents** and click **OK**.

*Session
window
output*

Tabulated Statistics

```
Rows: Smokes        Columns: Activity

                0       1       2       3      All

        1   100.00   33.33   31.15   23.81    30.43
        2      --     66.67   68.85   76.19    69.57
       All  100.00  100.00  100.00  100.00   100.00


    Cell Contents --
                    % of Col
```

Interpreting the results

The rows are the Smokes variable: the 1's are those who smoke regularly while the 2's are those who do not. The columns are activity level: 1 = slight, 2 = moderate, and 3 = a lot (the 0 activity level is there because a value was entered by mistake by the person who recorded the measurements). A third of the slightly active students smoke while only a fourth of the very active smoke. Further analysis would be necessary to test whether there is evidence that this is a significant difference.

Quality Control

MINITAB offers a wide variety of quality control methods: control charts and quality planning tools.

Control charts, or statistical process control (SPC) charts, allow you to study the variation of a process over time. These charts plot a summary statistic (for example, a sample mean or a sample proportion) against the sample number.

The commonly-used $\overline{X}$-R chart is shown on the following page. As the name suggests, that chart is actually two charts in the same Graph window: a control chart for subgroup means (an $\overline{X}$ chart) and a control chart for the subgroup ranges (an R chart). Seeing both charts together allows you to track both the process level and process variation at the same time, as well as detect the presence of special causes.

Subgroup data must be structured in a single column. When you have subgroups of unequal size, structure the subgroups in a single column, then set up a second column of subgroup identifiers.

▶ **To create an X̄-R chart**

1 Choose **Stat ➤ Control Charts ➤ Xbar-R**.

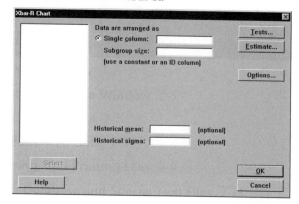

2 Enter the data column in **Single column**. In **Subgroup size**, enter a subgroup size or column of subgroup indicators.

3 If you like, use any of the options listed below, then click **OK**.

Options

- enter historical values for μ (the mean of the population distribution) and σ (the standard deviation of the population distribution) when you have a goal for μ or σ, or known parameters from prior data

- control the way MINITAB estimates μ or σ

- do eight tests for special causes

▷ **Example of an X̄ and R chart**

A manufacturing plant that makes metal fasteners needs to evaluate their ability to keep their process on target (2.4 grams) with minimal variation in the weight of the fasteners. The fasteners are packaged in batches of five. They randomly selected 20 bags of fasteners and drew an X̄ and R chart to evaluate the control of their production process.

1 Open the file FASTENER.MTW.

2 Choose **Stat ➤ Control Charts ➤ Xbar-R**.

3 In **Single column**, enter *Weights*. In **Subgroup size**, type 5.

4 In **Historical mean**, enter 2.4. Click **OK**.

Session window output

```
Test Results for Xbar Chart
TEST 1. One point more than 3.00 sigmas from center line.
Test Failed at points: 10
```

Graph window output

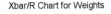

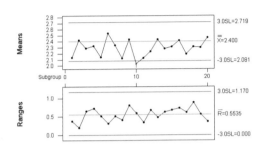

Interpreting the results

The test for special causes indicates that only one bag had a mean weight that was below the lower specification limit (3 standard deviations below the target value). However, you will notice that many of the points fall below the center line suggesting that the process is creating fasteners that are often below the target value. The plant's quality control engineer may want to perform additional tests for special causes and re-evaluate this process.

None of the subgroup ranges are out of control.

What Next?

This chapter barely scratched the surface of MINITAB's analysis capabilities. You also have access to a host of procedures in a wide range of statistical areas: nonparametrics, time series, and graphical analyses.

Some procedures in these areas are discussed in the sample sessions elsewhere in this book.

For complete details on other procedures, see Help.

5

Graphing Data

Graphing Data Overview

In MINITAB, you can work with graphs in many ways:

- **Create graphs** from the graph menu commands or from options in analysis commands. You can create any one of three types of graphs.

- **Manage the graphs** in Graph windows. Each graph is displayed in a separate Graph window. You can have up to 100 Graph windows open at once. The **Window** menu lists each one, and the Manage Graphs dialog box lets you rename, arrange, and discard graphs.

- **Edit the graphs** with point-and-click ease, using the variety of options on the Tool and Attribute palettes. You can change almost every aspect of the graph's appearance.

- **Brush the data points in graphs** to see the corresponding values from the worksheet. This is a great way to interactively discover the meaning of your data.

- **Save and print the graphs** the way you would any MINITAB window. When you save your project, all open Graph windows are saved along with it. You can also save graphs individually, in a variety of formats. Or, you can copy and paste graphs into other applications.

Tip | There are lots of graph examples in this book and in Help.

Three Types of Graphs

You can create three types of MINITAB graphs: Core Graphs, Specialty Graphs, and Character Graphs.

Graph type	Definition	Graphs
Core	The most common, simple types of graphs, such as scatter plots and charts, that can also use a variety of options to create a virtually unlimited number of two-dimensional graphs. For example, the Plot command can create a simple scatter plot, but you can change options to create line plots, area plots, projection plots, and more.	On the Graph menu: Plots Time series plots Charts Histograms Boxplots Matrix plots Draftsman plots

Graph type	Definition	Graphs
Specialty	"Pre-customized" graphs that automatically combine elements from core graphs to display data in unique or sophisticated ways. Some specialty graphs can be generated simply by selecting a checkbox in an analysis dialog box.	On the Graph menu: Dotplots Pie charts Marginal plots Probability plots On various menus: Interval plots Forecasting plots and more...
Character	"Typewriter-style" graphs formed from characters that display in the Session window.	On the Graph menu: Stem-and-leaf plots

In this chapter, you will see how to create a few core and speciality graphs. For more information on other graphs, see Help.

Creating Core Graphs

MINITAB's core graph commands let you easily create simple, common graphs. From that simple core you can add on a wide variety of graphics options to create complex, sophisticated graphs.

One of the most common and useful graphs is the scatter plot, which is created in MINITAB with the core graph command Plot. Below are the instructions for creating a basic scatter plot, followed by instructions on using some graphics options. Finally, there is an example of creating a scatter plot using those graphics options.

▶ **To create a basic scatter plot**

1 Choose **Graph ➤ Plot**.

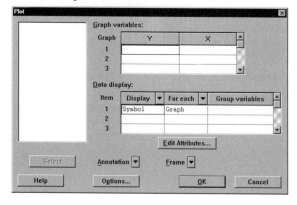

2 In first cell under **Y**, enter a variable.

3 In first cell under **X**, enter a variable. Click **OK**.

Data display elements and attributes

Data display elements are the graphical objects that represent data, such as symbols, bars, and connection lines. For example, in a scatter plot, each data point is represented by a symbol; on charts and histograms, each category is represented by a bar. In core graphs, you can change which data display elements to use on the graph. In the other types of graphs, many of the data display elements are already chosen for you.

Each data display element has *attributes*, such as size and color. You can change the attributes for all the data display elements in a graph, such as changing all the symbols to red. Core graphs offer you a lot of control over the appearance of data display elements.

▶ To change the appearance of data display elements

1 In a core graph dialog box, in the **Data display** table, click in the row of the element you want to affect.

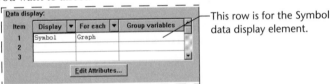

—This row is for the Symbol data display element.

2 Click **Edit Attributes**. Change the settings for that data display element. For example, here is the Edit Attributes dialog box for symbols:

3 Click **OK**.

Displaying data differently for each group

You can also change the attributes for a group of data display elements, such as making all the data points that have a certain value red, and all the data points that have another value blue. In a core graph main dialog box, you specify a *grouping variable*— a column which contains a list of values. MINITAB will create a different set of attributes for each unique value in that grouping variable. See *Example of a scatter plot with symbols in different colors* below.

▶ **To make one group appear differently than another**

1 In a core graph dialog box, in the **Data display** table, click in the row of the element you want to affect.

2 Next to **For each**, click the drop-down list and select **Group**.

3 Under **Group variables**, enter a variable.

▷ **Example of a scatter plot with symbols in different colors**

Say that you want to plot total sales figures versus advertising expenses. You would like to easily see how the expenses differ for each year. In the marketing data set (MARKET.MTW), the sales figures and advertising expenses are in the columns Sales and Advertis, and the year in which those expenses occurred (1991 or 1992) is in the column Year. By using Year as a grouping variable, you will make the data points that occurred in 1991 appear as black solid circles, and the 1992 points as yellow solid circles.

1 Open the file MARKET.MTW.

2 Choose **Graph ➤ Plot**.

3 In **Y**, enter *Sales*. In **X**, enter *Advertis*.

4 In the **Data display** table, choose **For each ➤ Group**.

5 Under **Group variables**, enter *Year*.

6 Click **Edit Attributes**.

7 First change all the symbols to use the same symbol type:
- Click the **Type** column header. This highlights all the rows in that column.
- Next to the **Type** column header, click the drop-down list and choose **Solid Circle**. Both rows will change at once.

8 Change 1992 circles to yellow:
- Under **Color**, click in the second row.
- From the **Color** drop-down list, choose **Yellow**.

9 Make the circle symbols twice as big:
- Click the **Size** column header. This highlights all the rows in that column.
- From the **Size** drop-down list, choose **2.0**. Both rows will change at once.

10 Click **OK** twice.

Graph window output

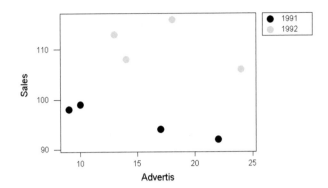

Creating Specialty Graphs

Using the core graph commands, you could create an incredible variety of two-dimensional graphs. The drawback is that for a complex graph, you might have to follow a large number of steps. With specialty graphs, the work is already done for you. The specialty graph commands let you specify just a few options to create useful, complex graphs.

Specialty graphs can be accessed in three ways:

- **On the Graph menu**. Specialty graphs that are applicable in a variety of statistical areas are found on the Graph menu.

- **On analysis menus**. Specialty graphs that are most often applicable to a single statistical area are found on the menu for that area. For example, residuals plots are often used in regression, so the command is accessed using the menu command **Stat ➤ Regression ➤ Residual Plots**.

- **As graph options in analysis dialog boxes**. Many graphs are created using the results of an analysis. Instead of storing results in the worksheet, then generating a graph from a menu command, often you can choose to display the graph as part of the analysis results. For example, when you perform a balanced analysis of variance, you can choose to create a histogram of the residuals and several other graphs: just open the Balanced Analysis of Variance dialog box, click **Graphs**, and select one or more graphs. When you execute the command, MINITAB will display text output in the Session window, and display the requested graphs in Graph windows.

▶ **To create a marginal plot**

The Marginal Plot command makes it easy to create a scatter plot that has another type of graph, such as a histogram, placed in the margins.

Example of a marginal plot with histograms

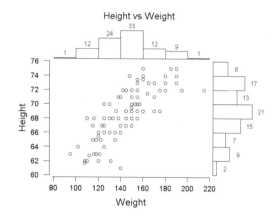

1   Choose **Graph ➤ Marginal Plot**.

2   Enter one column in **Y variable** and one column in **X variable**.

3   Under **Type of marginal plot**, choose **Histogram, Boxplot,** or **Dotplot**. Click **OK**.

Managing Graph Windows

You can have up to 100 Graph windows open at once. MINITAB provides a handy tool for arranging, naming, opening, and closing multiple Graph windows: the Manage Graphs dialog box.

▶ **To manage graphs**

1   Choose **Window ➤ Manage Graphs**.

You can control many graphs at once: just highlight the graphs in the list and click a button.

2 In the **Graphs** list box, select one or more graphs.

3 Click any of the action buttons. The action will be applied to all the selected graphs, one at a time if necessary. For example, **Tile** arranges all the selected graphs at once; **Save As** tells MINITAB to prompt you to save each graph, one at a time.

4 Click any of the other action buttons. When you are finished, click **Done**.

Graph Editing

After you produce a graph in a Graph window, you can edit it. Graph editing is useful for putting text, lines, marker symbols, and polygons anywhere on an existing graph. You can also edit and change the attributes of objects generated with the existing graph. The graph editing tools, shown below, are often easier to use than the graph's options dialog boxes.

Use the Tool palette to create text, rectangles, ovals, lines, markers, and open and closed polygons.

Use the Attribute palette to change the color, size, and type of objects on the graph. You can change text, edges, fills, and symbols.

Note, however, that the changes you make with graph editing tools apply only to that particular Graph window, and do not affect the settings in the dialog box that created the graph. That means that if your data changes and you want to create a new graph, any changes you made to the first graph with graph editing tools would not be carried over.

For example, say that you create a plot with the Plot dialog box, then use the graph editing features to change all the plot's symbols from black to red. When you open the Plot dialog box again, the symbol attributes will still be set to black; when you click **OK**, a second Graph window will appear that contains a plot with black symbols.

▶ **To enter Edit mode**

1 Do one of the following:

  ■ Double-click the graph.

  ■ Make the Graph window active and choose **Editor ➤ Edit**.

Tip | When you enter Edit mode, the Tool and Attribute palettes should appear. If they do not, choose **Editor ➤ Show Tool Palette** or **Editor ➤ Show Attribute Palette**.

▶ To add a title

1 With the Graph window in Edit mode, click on the Text tool.

2 Drag an area where you want your title.

3 The Text box automatically appears. Type your title and click **OK**.

For example, you could add a title to the graph created on page 5-5.

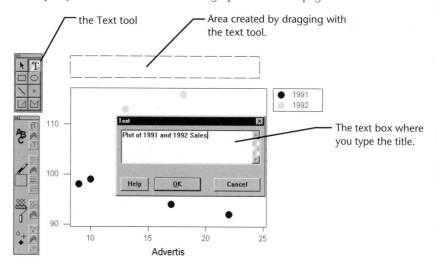

the Text tool

Area created by dragging with the text tool.

The text box where you type the title.

▶ To change the title size

1 With the Graph window in Edit mode, click on the title of the graph.

2 On the Attribute palette, click the Size tool.

3 Pick a size from the menu.

More | Graph editing commands provide you with a full set of drawing, text, and coloring tools to modify your graphs as you wish when a graph is your active window.

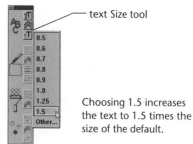

text Size tool

Choosing 1.5 increases the text to 1.5 times the size of the default.

Brushing Graphs

Graphs allow you to visually see the relationships between points. However, after you make a graph, you often want to learn more about a point, or a group of points. Brushing allows you to highlight points on a graph and see the corresponding observations (rows) in the Brushing palette and in the Data window.

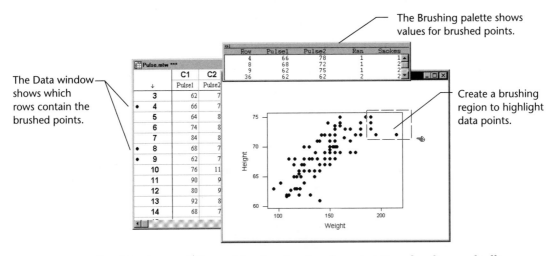

The Brushing palette shows values for brushed points.

The Data window shows which rows contain the brushed points.

Create a brushing region to highlight data points.

Brushing is especially good for showing the characteristics of outliers and telling whether points that lie in a brushing region share other characteristics.

Note | Some graphs cannot be brushed. You can only brush graphs that use symbols to represent individual data points, such as scatter plots or time series plots. Some specialty graphs also cannot be brushed because the symbols represent data that was created temporarily by the command; the data does not exist in the worksheet.

▶ **To brush a graph**

1 Make the Graph window active.

2 Choose **Editor ➤ Brush**.

3 Drag the ⬅ cursor over the points in the graph.

▶ **To add columns to the Brushing palette**

1 Choose **Editor ➤ Set ID Variables**.

2 Click **Use columns** and type the column names or numbers you want to display. Click **OK**.

Printing and Saving Graphs

Printing graphs

You can print a graph just as you would any other MINITAB window.

▶ **To print a graph**

1 With the Graph window active, choose **File ➤ Print Graph**.

Saving graphs

Saving the contents of a Graph window is similar to saving other MINITAB windows. When you save your project, all open graphs are saved as part of the project (see *Opening, saving, and closing projects* on page 1-8). You can also save or export graphs individually. The method you pick depends on your needs:

- If you want to view and edit that graph in other MINITAB projects, or if you want to view the graph in earlier releases of MINITAB, save the graph in a MINITAB Graphics Format (MGF) file. You can then re-open that graph in MINITAB.

- If you want to use the graph in another application, such as in Microsoft Word or on a web page, you can save the graph in a file format such as bitmap (BMP) or JPEG (JPG).

- If you want to view *and* edit that graph in other Windows applications, you can copy and paste the graph. The graph is an OLE (pronounced "o lay") object that can be edited with MINITAB graph editing tools within the other application.

- If you want the graph to appear in a printed word processing document at the highest-possible resolution, you can print the graph to an Encapsulated PostScript (EPS) file. This creates an image that cannot be viewed in the word processing program, but will print at the best quality. For details, see Help.

▶ **To save a graph**

1 With the Graph window active, choose **File ➤ Save Graph As**.

2 In **Save as type**, choose the format that can be used by the other application. To use the graph in MINITAB, choose *Minitab Graph*.

3 In **File name**, type a name and click **Save**.

▶ **To open a graph**

You can open a MINITAB Graphics Format (MGF) file, or open graphs that are contained in a MINITAB Project (MPJ) file.

1 Choose **File ➤ Open Graph**.

2 Under **Files of type**, select either MINITAB Graphics Format or MINITAB Project.

3 Select a directory and file name, then click **Open**.

4 If you select a MINITAB Project file, Minitab then displays a list of the graphs in that project. Select a graph and click **OK**.

▶ **To copy and paste a graph**

1 With the Graph window active, choose **Edit ➤ Copy Graph**.

2 In the other application, choose the paste command.

Note | If the application is OLE compliant, the graph will be pasted as an OLE object you can edit with the MINITAB graph editor (below). If the application is not OLE compliant, the graph will be pasted as a Windows Metafile. Depending on the capabilities of the application, the Metafile will be pasted as a drawing whose parts (titles, lines, symbols, etc.) can be individually edited by that application's editing tools, or as a static bitmap.

▶ **To edit a pasted MINITAB graph in another application**

This option is only available if the application is OLE compliant.

1 Double-click the graph. The MINITAB graph editing window will appear.

2 Use MINITAB's graph editing tools.

3 Close the window. The changes will be reflected in the application.

Tip | With the OLE graph editor, you can also save a copy of the graph to a file: choose **File ➤ Save Copy As**.

6

Managing the Session Window and Generating Reports

Overview

The Session window displays the text output generated by your analyses.

output title

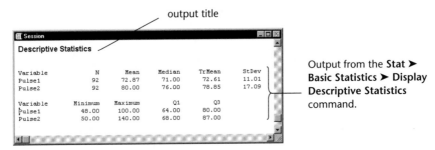

Output from the **Stat ➤ Basic Statistics ➤ Display Descriptive Statistics** command.

In the Session window you can

- navigate through the output (which can add up when you use the same project for a long time)

- edit and format text

- print and save text in different file formats (Session window text can then be used in a word processor or some other application)

More | The Session window can also display the command language used to generate the output, as well as provide a place to type session commands. For details on both these features, see *Executing Session Commands* on page 7-2.

Navigating in the Session Window

To view output, you can use the Session window scroll bars or use arrow keys just as you would in any window on your system. MINITAB also offers other ways to find output: the **Next Command** and **Previous Command** buttons let you jump to the output for each command, and the **Find** command lets you search for specific words or numbers in your output.

▶ **To move to command output**

1 To move forward (down) to the next block of output, click the ⬇ button on the Session window toolbar or choose **Editor ➤ Next Command**.

2 To move backward (up) to the previous block of output, click the ⬆ button on the Session window toolbar or choose **Editor ➤ Previous Command**.

▶ **To find words or numbers**

1 With the Session window active, choose **Editor ➤ Find**.

2 In **Find what**, type the characters you want to search for.

3 Click **Find Next**.

More | MINITAB also has a feature for automatically replacing text—see *Finding and replacing text* on page 6-5.

Editing and Formatting Text

To do any editing or formatting in the Session window, you must first make the output editable (described below). Then you can do any of the following:

- Select text

- Change text or add comments

- Cut, copy, or paste text to other parts of the Session window, to the Data window, or to other applications

- Find and replace text

More | You can also change the fonts used in the Session window. For details, see Help.

Making output editable or read-only

The Session window is by default set to Read-Only. This means that output can be copied, but it cannot be deleted or modified. If you want to add comments, cut and paste text and numbers, or use the Replace feature (see *Finding and replacing text* on page 6-5), you can change the Session window to Editable.

▶ **To change editing modes**

You can change modes back and forth throughout a session.

- To set the Session window to Editable, choose **Editor ➤ Make Output Editable**. If the Editor menu says **Make Output Read-Only**, you do not have to do anything.

- To set the Session window to Read-Only, choose **Editor ➤ Make Output Read-Only**. If the Editor menu says **Make Output Editable**, you do not have to do anything.

Selecting text

As well as the standard ways to select text in a Windows environment (such as dragging the mouse or using [Shift] + a navigation key), the Session window offers three other methods that you may find useful:

▶ **To select...**   **Do this**

To select...	Do this
all the text in the Session window	Choose **Edit ➤ Select All**.
an entire line or group of lines	Drag along the left margin.
a rectangle (or column)	While holding down [Alt], drag the mouse to form a rectangle.

Tip | The rectangle selection option is especially useful for copying columnar output to paste into the Data window or a spreadsheet. For details, see *To copy Session window output to the Data window* on page 6-5.

Editing text

You can change and add text in the Session window just as you would in a Windows word processor.

▶ **To edit text in the Session window**

- To delete text, select the text, then press [Delete].

- To insert blank lines, press [Enter].

- To add comments, position the cursor wherever you want and type.

Note | If the comment is on a line by itself (and not on a line of output, or a line containing a title), the text will be in the comment font. For details on using fonts, see Help.

Cutting, copying, and pasting

You can cut, copy, and paste text just as you would in a word processor. You can exchange text with other applications, delete or move text in the Session window, or copy Session window output to the Data window.

When you copy text to the Clipboard, the text is copied in two formats: Text (ASCII or TXT), which has no fonts, and Rich Text Format (RTF), which retains fonts. If you paste into an application that understands RTF, the output will appear exactly as it does in MINITAB. If you paste into an application that does not understand RTF, the plain text will be pasted.

| Tip | With plain text, the tables of output may not line up correctly in the other application. To make the output appear as it does in MINITAB, apply a monospace font, such as Courier. |

▶ To copy Session window output to the Data window

1   Highlight the desired text in the Session window. To select a rectangle of output, hold down the [Alt] key while dragging with the mouse.

2   Choose **Edit ➤ Copy**.

3   In a Data window, place your cursor in the cell that is the top left corner of the area you want to paste to. Make sure there is enough room for the selection in the surrounding cells. If there is not enough room, the pasted data will overwrite the existing data.

Rectangular selection that is two columns wide and three rows long.

There is enough room to the right and below the active cell to paste the selection.

4   Choose **Edit ➤ Paste**.

5   A dialog box appears. Click one of the following buttons:

   ■ To paste the data across columns (one value in the first column, one value in the next column, etc.), click **Use spaces as delimiters**.

   ■ To paste all the data in one column, click **Paste as a single column**.

Finding and replacing text

▶ To find and replace text

1   Choose **Editor ➤ Replace**.

2   In **Find what**, type the text you want to search for. In **Replace with**, type the replacement text. You can type any combination of numbers and letters, such as "Jabberwocky9."

3   Click **Find Next**.

4   If the text you want to replace is found, click **Replace** or **Replace All**. If you do not want to replace this particular item, click **Find Next**.

Printing and Saving Text

Your session consists of everything you see in the Session window, such as tables of statistical results and comments you may have added. You can print all of the Session window or just a portion of it. You can also save the Session window text in different file formats.

Printing the Session window

▶ To print the entire window

1 Make the window active.

2 Choose **File ➤ Print Session Window** and click **OK**.

▶ To print a block of text

1 Select text in the Session window.

2 Choose **File ➤ Print Session Window**.

3 Under **Print Range**, make sure **Selection** is chosen. Click **OK**.

Saving Session window contents

You can save the Session window contents in several formats.

▶ To save the contents of the Session window

1 Make the Session window active.

2 Choose **File ➤ Save Session Window As**.

3 Under **Files of type**, pick a file type:

- Text (TXT) file—a plain text file that does not contain fonts, but is understood by every word processor and text editor.

- Rich Text Format (RTF) file—a format that retains fonts and is understood by many word processors.

- List (LIS) file—useful for longtime users of MINITAB, this option creates a plain text file with the extension LIS. The OUTFILE session command saves Session text with an LIS extension, and this option lets you create an identical outfile without using session commands.

4 Enter a name and click **OK**.

7

Session Commands and Execs

Session Commands and Execs Overview

Session commands are a useful alternative to menu commands, especially when you want to repeat a group of actions or create an Exec.

What are session commands? Whenever you use a menu command, or click OK in a dialog box, MINITAB generates commands that describe the action. Most commands are simple, easy to remember words, like PLOT, CHART, or SORT. These session commands, collectively referred to as *command language*, are stored in the History window.

You can execute session commands to carry out actions immediately. Commands can be entered in two places: the Command Line Editor and the Session window. If you want to repeat a group of actions, you can copy commands from the History window and paste them into the Command Line Editor or Session window.

If the group of commands are ones you want to repeat often, you can create an Exec. An Exec file can be saved, shared with others, and executed whenever you want.

If you use session commands often, you will probably want to enable command language in the Session window. This will let you see the session commands along with your text output, and will also let you type session commands in the Session window.

Executing Session Commands

You can type commands in two places: the Command Line Editor and the Session window. The Command Line Editor is more convenient, but long-time users of MINITAB may be used to typing commands in the Session window.

▶ **To execute commands with the Command Line Editor**

1   Choose **Edit ➤ Command Line Editor**.

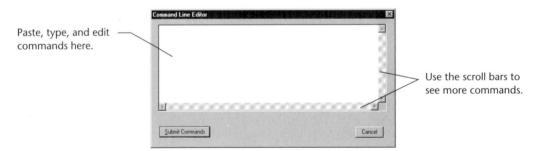

Paste, type, and edit commands here.

Use the scroll bars to see more commands.

2   Type the session commands—see *Basic Rules for Typing Session Commands* below.

3   Click **Submit Commands**.

▶ **To execute commands in the Session window**

1 Make the Session window active.

2 Choose **Editor ➤ Enable Command Language**. If the Editor menu shows Disable Command Language, you do not have to do anything.

3 Type the session commands at the MTB > prompt—see *Basic Rules for Typing Session Commands* below.

4 After each command or subcommand line, press Enter.

▶ **To repeat a block of commands**

1 Choose **Window ➤ History**.

2 Select the block of commands and choose **Edit ➤ Copy**.

3 In the Command Line Editor, or at the Session window's MTB > prompt, press Ctrl+V.

4 In the Command Line Editor, click **Submit Commands**. In the Session window, press Enter.

More | To work through an example of quickly repeating an analysis using this method, see Chapter 10, *Session Three: Advanced MINITAB*.

▶ **To show session commands along with output**

1 Choose **Editor ➤ Enable Command Language**. If the Editor menu shows Disable Command Language, you do not have to do anything.

Basic Rules for Typing Session Commands

Command order and punctuation

Type commands in this order:

1 Type the main command, followed by any arguments. If you are going to use subcommands, end the main command line with a semicolon.

2 Type any subcommands and any subcommand arguments, ending each line with a semicolon.

3 With the last subcommand, end the line with a period.

Specifying arguments

Arguments can be variables (columns and stored constants), text strings, or numbers (constants).

Variables

- Enclose variable names in single quotation marks (for example, HISTOGRAM 'Salary').

- Variable names and variable numbers are interchangeable. For example, the two following commands do the same thing (if C1 is named 'Sales'):
  ```
  DESCRIBE C1 C2
  DESCRIBE 'Sales' C2
  ```

- Specify a range of variables by using a hyphen between the first and last variables you want. For example, PRINT C2–C5 is equivalent to PRINT C2 C3 C4 C5. If C2 was named Sales and C5 was named Costs, you could also type PRINT 'Sales'-'Costs'.

Text strings and numbers

- enclose text strings (such as file names or titles) in double quotes, as in TITLE "This Is My Title"

- do not enclose numbers in quotes unless you want the number to appear as text.

- To specify a range of numbers, abbreviate a sequence by using the following conventions:

1:4	expands to 1 2 3 4
4:1	expands to 4 3 2 1
1:3/.5	expands to 1 1.5 2 2.5 3

More | For more options and syntax variations of session commands, see the Session command Help file.

Using Execs

Execs are simply collections of commands that execute one after another, and work as long as the input data are always in the same columns and the output data can go in the same columns. This section discusses how to create and invoke Execs.

Creating an Exec

▶ To create an Exec

1 Perform your analysis, using menu commands or session commands as you prefer.

2 In the History window, select the desired session commands and choose **Edit ➤ Copy**.

3 Open a text editor, such as Windows Notepad. Paste the text.

4 Save the file as any name with the extension MTB, as in MYEXEC.MTB.

   If you are using a word processor, make sure to save the file as plain text (ASCII or TXT format); do not use the word processor's native format.

▶ To invoke an Exec

1 Open the worksheet that contains the data that will work with that Exec.

2 Choose **File ➤ Other Files ➤ Run an Exec**.

An Exec can run once, or many times. "1" appears by default.

3 Click **Select File**.

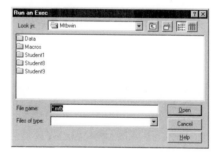

4 Select the directory and file you want. Click **Open**. The Exec will run.

8

Session One: MINITAB Basics

Chapter 8

Overview of Session One

The story

Clones are genetically identical cells descended from the same individual. Researchers have identified a single poplar clone that yields fast-growing, hardy trees. These trees may one day be an alternative energy resource to conventional fuel.

Researchers at The Pennsylvania State University planted Poplar Clone 252 on two different sites—one, a site by a creek with rich, well-drained soil; the other, a site on a ridge with dry, sandy soil. They measured the diameter in centimeters, height in meters, and dry weight of the wood in kilograms of a sample of three-year-old trees. These researchers want to see if they can predict how much a tree weighs from its diameter and height measurements.

Congratulations! You have been hired as data analyst for the project, and you will be performing the statistical analysis.

What you will learn

In Session One you will learn how to:

- open a worksheet
- enter and edit data
- save data
- compute some basic statistics
- do arithmetic

- plot the data
- compute a correlation coefficient
- edit and add comments to the output
- print and save your results

Time required

About 20 minutes.

Step 1: Start MINITAB

The way you start MINITAB depends on which operating system you are using.

- To start in Windows 95 or Windows NT 4.0:
  From the Taskbar, choose **Start ➤ Programs ➤ Minitab Student 12 ➤ Minitab**.

- To start in Windows NT 3.51:
  Locate and open the Minitab 12 for Windows program group, then double-click the Minitab icon ⊒ .

Step 2: Open a Worksheet

When you start MINITAB, you begin with a new, empty project. You can add data to your project in many ways, but the most common way is to open a worksheet. Note that you are only copying the data from the worksheet to the project; any changes that you make to the data added to your project will not affect the original file.

In this session, you will use the file POPLAR1.MTW. This file is one of the dozens of worksheets that are shipped with MINITAB. Most of these worksheets are in the DATA subdirectory or folder.

1 Choose **File ➤ Open Worksheet**.

2 Make sure the file type is Minitab (*.mtw) and the current subdirectory is DATA.

3 Click on POPLAR1.MTW and click **Open**.

4 If the Data window is not already visible, open it to view the columns in your worksheet: choose **Window ➤ POPLAR1.MTW** or press Ctrl + D.

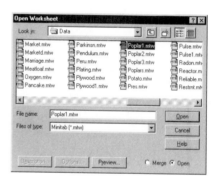

This worksheet contains three variables, labeled Diameter, Height, and Weight. Each variable contains 15 observations—all the data collected so far.

	C1	C2	C3	C4	C5	C6	C7
↓	Diameter	Height	Weight				
1	0.23	3.76	0.17				
2	2.12	3.15	0.15				
3	1.06	1.85	0.02				
4	2.12	3.64	0.16				
5	2.99	4.64	0.37				
6	4.01	5.25	0.73				
7	2.41	4.07	0.22				

Step 3: Enter Data from the Keyboard

The worksheet POPLAR1 contained the data collected so far, but you just received new observations from the field, and there are five new rows to enter.

1 Press ⬇ until you reach the first blank cell in row 16 or, with your mouse, click on the first blank cell in row 16.

The Data window should look like this:

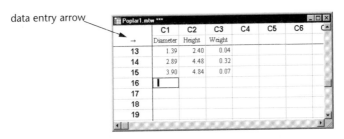

data entry arrow

2 Make sure the data entry arrow points to the right. If it does not, click on it to change its direction.

3 Type the following from left to right across each row:

1.52	Enter	2.9	Enter	.07	Ctrl + Enter
4.51	Enter	5.27	Enter	.79	Ctrl + Enter
1.18	Enter	2.2	Enter	.03	Ctrl + Enter
3.17	Enter	4.93	Enter	.44	Ctrl + Enter
3.33	Enter	4.89	Enter	.52	Ctrl + Enter

> **Tip** | **If you make a mistake:** click on or move to a cell (the contents will be automatically selected), type the correct value, and press Enter.

Step 4: Enter Patterned Data

You can always type data in the Data window, but if your data follow a pattern, there is an easier way to enter your data.

You now want to create a new variable that will indicate whether an observation was taken from the site with rich, well-drained soil (1), or from the site with dry, sandy soil (2). This new variable, called Site, will contain ten 1's followed by ten 2's.

1 Choose **Calc ➤ Make Patterned Data ➤ Simple Set of Numbers**.

2 To store the new data: in **Store patterned data in**, type *Site*. MINITAB will automatically assign this new variable to the first empty column—in this case, C4.

3 To indicate the beginning and end of the sequence: in **From first value**, type *1*; In **To last value**, type *2*.

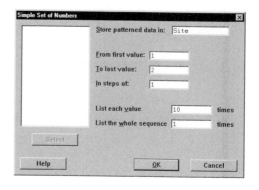

4 Since you want ten 1's and ten 2's, in **List each value**, type *10*. Then click **OK**.

The new Site column appears in the Data and Info windows:

To open the Info window, choose **Window ➤ Info** or press Ctrl+I.

Step 5: Save Your Project

It is a good idea to save your work frequently. Now is probably a good time to save, since you have just entered new data.

1 Choose **File ➤ Save Project**.

2 In **File name**, enter *POPLAR1* for the name of your project. If you omit the extension .MPJ, MINITAB will automatically add it once you save the document.

3 Click **Save**.

4 If you see a message box asking if you want to replace an existing file, click **Yes**.

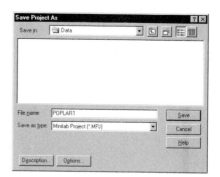

Step 6: Compute Descriptive Statistics

MINITAB offers a wide array of basic statistics to help you analyze your data, such as descriptive statistics, t-tests, z-tests, and correlations. You decide to produce a separate summary table for the trees at each site describing the three variables Diameter, Height, and Weight.

1 Choose **Stat ➤ Basic Statistics ➤ Display Descriptive Statistics**.

2 In the variable list box, click *Diameter* and drag the mouse so that you highlight *Diameter*, *Height*, and *Weight*. Then click **Select**.

3 Check **By variable**, and enter *Site*.

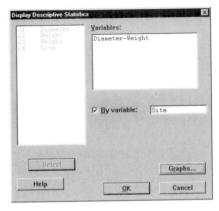

Checking **By variable** tells MINITAB to generate separate statistics for Diameter, Height, and Weight for each level of the variable Site.

Note | When you select a series of columns, MINITAB uses a dash to abbreviate the series. In this example, Diameter–Weight means the variables Diameter, Height, and Weight.

4 Click **Graphs**.

5 Check **Boxplot of data** and click **OK** twice.

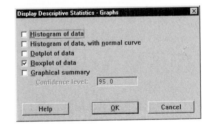

MINITAB displays text output in the Session window and each graph (three, in this case) in its own Graph window.

Session window output

Descriptive Statistics

Variable	Site	N	Mean	Median	TrMean	StDev
Diameter	1	10	2.598	2.320	2.604	0.916
	2	10	3.028	3.250	3.041	1.284
Height	1	10	4.098	4.120	4.175	1.103
	2	10	4.255	4.865	4.351	1.254
Weight	1	10	0.3090	0.2050	0.2862	0.2528
	2	10	0.399	0.380	0.356	0.366

Variable	Site	SE Mean	Minimum	Maximum	Q1	Q3
Diameter	1	0.290	1.060	4.090	2.120	3.245
	2	0.406	1.180	4.770	1.487	4.053
Height	1	0.349	1.850	5.730	3.517	4.852
	2	0.396	2.200	5.540	2.775	5.142
Weight	1	0.0800	0.0200	0.7800	0.1575	0.4600
	2	0.116	0.030	1.110	0.062	0.647

*Graph
window
output*

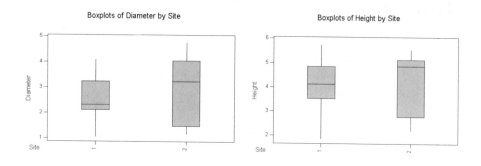

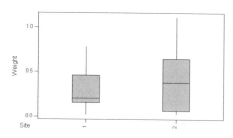

Tip | Tile the graphs to view all of them at one time on your screen. Choose **Window ➤ Manage Graphs**, select the graphs you want, and click **Tile**. When the graphs are finished tiling, click **Done**.

Judging from the boxplots, Site 2 is producing larger trees than Site 1. The Session window output contains the details: all three variables show larger means and medians at Site 2. Also, the variable Weight has a very large standard deviation relative to its size. At Site 2, the minimum weight is only 0.03 kg while the maximum is 1.11 kg. It appears that some of our poplars are doing very well, while others are barely alive.

Step 7: Perform Arithmetic

Now on to the task of predicting how much the trees weigh. Based on previous work, the researchers have found that the weight of a tree is closely related to the square of diameter, multiplied by height. Since you have diameter and height data, you can calculate this new variable using MINITAB's calculator. The calculator performs the equation you enter and puts the result in the variable you specify.

1 Choose **Calc ➤ Calculator**.

2 You decide to call the new variable "D2H" for diameter squared times height. In **Store result in variable**, type *D2H*.

3 In **Expression**, type *C1**2*C2*. Click **OK**.

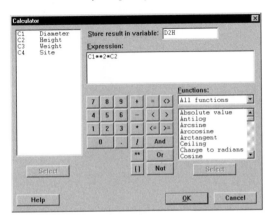

This expression tells MINITAB to square the variable Diameter (C1), multiply by the variable Height (C2), and put the result in a new variable called D2H.

Tip   You could also use the mouse to create the equation: (1) select *Diameter* from the variable list, (2) click the **, 2, and * buttons on the calculator, and (3) select *Height* from the variable list.

The Data window shows the new variable D2H that you just created:

	C1	C2	C3	C4	C5	C6	C7
	Diameter	Height	Weight	Site	D2H		
1	2.23	3.76	0.17	1	18.698		
2	2.12	3.15	0.15	1	14.157		
3	1.06	1.85	0.02	1	2.079		
4	2.12	3.64	0.16	1	16.360		
5	2.99	4.64	0.37	1	41.482		
6	4.01	5.25	0.73	1	84.421		
7	2.41	4.07	0.22	1	23.639		

Poplar1.mtw ***

Now save the project changes.

4 Choose **File ➤ Save Project**, or press Ctrl+S.

Step 8: Create a Scatter Plot

The researchers have determined that there is a relationship between weight and this variable called D2H. You want to see if your poplars' data exhibit this relationship as well by plotting Weight by D2H on a scatter plot:

1 Choose **Graph** ➤ **Plot**.

2 In **Y** (the vertical axis), enter *Weight*.

3 In **X** (the horizontal axis), enter *D2H* and click **OK**.

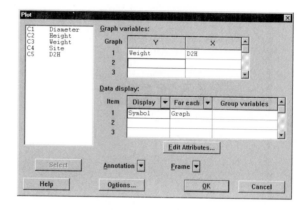

Graph window output

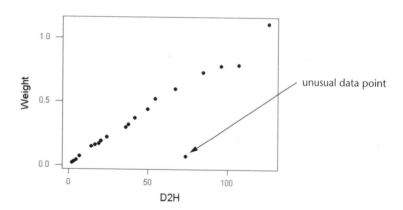

You see a positive linear relationship between Weight and D2H. That is, as D2H increases, so does Weight. You also notice an unusual data point—a tree that has a very low weight for a relatively high D2H value. For now, you decide to ignore it, but it is something you may want to check on later. Next, you will compute the correlation between these two variables to quantify the relationship.

Step 9: Compute a Correlation Coefficient

From the scatter plot, you have seen that as D2H increases, so does Weight. Now you want to measure the association between these two variables by computing a correlation coefficient.

1   Choose **Stat ➤ Basic Statistics ➤ Correlation**.

2   In **Variables**, enter *Weight* and *D2H*. Click OK.

Session window output

Correlations (Pearson)

```
Correlation of Weight and D2H = 0.913, P-Value = 0.000
```

The correlation coefficient measures the linear relationship between two variables and assumes a value between −1 and +1. The high positive correlation coefficient of 0.913 is close to 1, thus quantifying the relationship that you already saw in the scatter plot—there is a strong linear association between Weight and D2H (diameter squared times height) for the trees in our sample.

Step 10: Edit the Session Window Output

It is time to create a report of your results: the text results, such as the summary descriptive statistics you computed; and the graphs, such as the scatter plot.

First you will edit the text output in the Session window to make it more appropriate for a report. You can edit text in MINITAB's Session window similar to the way you can edit with a word processor, even finding and replacing text and changing fonts.

By default, the Session window is *read-only*, so that you cannot accidentally delete results. To begin editing, you will have to make the Session window editable:

1 Press Ctrl+M to make the Session window active.

2 Pull down the **Editor** menu.

3 There is a menu item that works like a toggle: it can read **Make Output Editable** or **Make Output Read-Only**:

- If the item reads **Make Output Editable**, click it.

- If the item reads **Make Output Read-Only**, do not do anything. You can click outside the menu to cancel it.

Now you can edit your output.

4 Delete all the text above the Descriptive Statistics output and all the text between the Descriptive Statistics output and the Correlation output. Select the text by dragging over it with your mouse, then delete it by choosing **Edit ➤ Cut** or pressing Delete.

5 Scroll to the top of the Session window and type four comment lines as shown below:

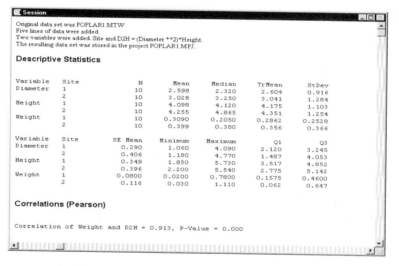

6 Save your work. Choose **File ➤ Save Project**.

The Session window is ready to print.

Step 11: Print Your Work

To print the contents of any window, switch to that window, then choose **File ➤ Print Session Window**. You will first print your output from the Session window, and then your graphs from the Graph windows.

1 Choose **File ➤ Print Session Window**, then click **OK**. Since you are in the Session window, that is what will be printed.

You could go to each Graph window and print them separately, but if you have more than one graph there is a faster way.

2 Choose **Window ➤ Manage Graphs**.

3 Select the four graphs you have created: click on **Boxplts of Diameter by Site** and drag down.

4 Click **Print**. Click **OK**.

5 When the graphs have printed, click **Done**.

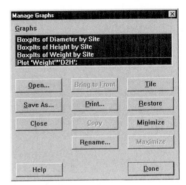

Step 12: Save Your Work

When you save your project, you save all your work at once: all the data, all the output in the Session window, and all the open Graph windows. When you reopen the project, all that information will be waiting for you, right where you left it.

1 Choose **File ➤ Save Project**.

More | If you want to use output or data in another application or another MINITAB project, you can save your Session window output, data, and graphs as separate files. These separate files are copies of what is currently in your project—the contents of your project are not changed in any way.

Step 13: Exit MINITAB

If you want to take a break before continuing to another session, you can exit MINITAB.

1 Choose **File ➤ Exit**.

2 MINITAB may ask if you want to save changes to your project. Since you already saved your project above, there is no need to do it again here. Click **No**.

9

Session Two: Doing a Simple Analysis

Overview of Session Two

The story

Researchers at The Pennsylvania State University planted hundreds of poplar trees and grew them under a variety of controlled conditions. After three years, they measured the diameter in centimeters, height in meters, and dry weight of the wood in kilograms of a sample of trees.

You believe there is a close relationship between the dry weight of wood from young poplar trees and a variable that is a function of the diameter and the height of the trees. But what is that relationship?

These fast-growing, hardy trees may one day serve as an alternative source of fuel or chemicals. As data analyst for the project, you will determine if diameter and height measurements can be used to reliably predict the yield of wood.

What you will learn

In this session, you learn how to:

- use simple regression to find the relationship between the trees' diameter and height
- find and correct errors in your data, then quickly re-run your analysis
- generate graphs to visualize the relationship between variables
- customize the appearance of those graphs to make them more informative
- brush the graphs to identify key data points

Time required

About 20 minutes.

Step 1: Start a New Project

- If you are not already running MINITAB, start the program.
- If you have just completed Session One, start a new project: choose **File ► New**, click **Minitab Project**, and click **OK**.

If you have not saved your changes to the previous project, MINITAB will give you the chance to do so.

Step 2: Open a Worksheet

You will get data from a MINITAB saved worksheet named POPLAR2.MTW that is located in the DATA subdirectory or folder.

1 Choose **File ➤ Open Worksheet**.

2 Move to the DATA subdirectory and select the file POPLAR2.MTW. Click **Open**.

Step 3: Perform a Simple Regression

Towards the end of Session One, you saw that as D2H increases, so does Weight. One way to find out how well D2H predicts weight is to use a simple regression command:

1 Choose **Stat ➤ Regression ➤ Regression**.

2 In **Response**, enter *Weight*.

3 In **Predictors**, enter *D2H*.

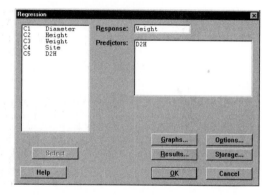

You decide you might as well do a series of plots for residual analysis to check for any potential problems.

4 Click **Graphs**.

5 Under **Residuals for Plots**, click **Standardized**.

6 Under **Residual Plots**, click **Histogram of residuals** and **Normal plot of residuals**.

7 In **Residuals versus the variables**, enter *D2H*.

8 Click **OK** twice.

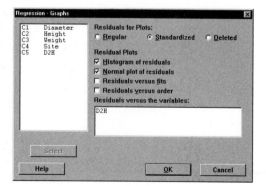

MINITAB displays the text output in the Session window, and displays each of the three graphs in its own Graph window.

*Session
window
output*

Regression Analysis

The regression equation is
Weight = 0.0196 + 0.00758 D2H

```
Predictor        Coef        StDev           T        P
Constant      0.01961      0.04566        0.43    0.673
D2H          0.0075838    0.0007994       9.49    0.000
```

S = 0.1298   R-Sq = 83.3%   R-Sq(adj) = 82.4%

Analysis of Variance

```
Source           DF          SS          MS           F        P
Regression        1      1.5155      1.5155       89.99    0.000
Residual Error   18      0.3031      0.0168
Total            19      1.8187
```

Unusual Observations
```
Obs      D2H     Weight         Fit   StDev Fit     Residual   St Resid
 12      126     1.1100      0.9756      0.0717       0.1344      1.24 X
 15       74     0.0700      0.5779      0.0374      -0.5079     -4.09R
```

R denotes an observation with a large standardized residual
X denotes an observation whose X value gives it large influence

*Graph
window
output*

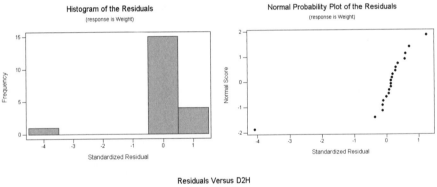

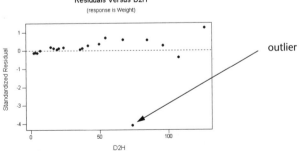

MINITAB displays the regression equation, the table of coefficients, the analysis of variance table, and—in the table of unusual observations—the identity of the outlier and influential observations (rows 12 and 15). Before proceeding with further analysis, you want to examine rows 12 and 15 to make sure they contain valid data.

A quick glance at the Residuals Versus D2H plot shows you that the data contains an outlier.

Step 4: Edit the Data

1 To view the worksheet, go to the Data window, choose **Window ➤ POPLAR2.MTW**, or press Ctrl+D.

2 Now go to the first unusual observation, in row 12 of the column named Weight:

- Choose **Editor ➤ Go To**.

- In the **Enter column number or name** box, type *Weight*.

- In the **Enter row number** box, type *12* and click **OK**.

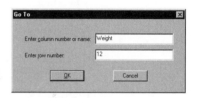

The Data window now shows the 12th observation of Weight as the highlighted cell.

	C1	C2	C3	C4	C5	C6	C7	C8
↓	Diameter	Height	Weight	Site	D2H			
7	2.41	4.07	0.22	1	23.639			
8	2.75	4.72	0.30	1	35.695			
9	2.20	4.17	0.19	1	20.183			
10	4.09	5.73	0.78	1	95.852			
11	3.62	5.10	0.60	2	66.832			
12	4.77	5.54	1.11	2	126.051			
13	1.39	2.40	0.04	2	4.637			

Both Weight and D2H seem rather large, so you double-check the researchers' log sheets. It turns out that poplar #12 is a very healthy tree—the values are correct.

3 Click on the Weight value in row 15 to highlight it, or press ↓ three times.

	C1	C2	C3	C4	C5	C6	C7	C8
↓	Diameter	Height	Weight	Site	D2H			
10	4.09	5.73	0.78	1	95.852			
11	3.62	5.10	0.60	2	66.832			
12	4.77	5.54	1.11	2	126.051			
13	1.39	2.40	0.04	2	4.637			
14	2.89	4.48	0.32	2	37.417			
15	3.90	4.84	0.07	2	73.616			
16	1.52	2.90	0.07	2	6.700			

Double-checking the log sheet shows that this value is actually an error. The correct value should be .70, not .07.

4 Type .7 and press Enter.

The Data window should look like this:

	C1	C2	C3	C4	C5	C6	C7	C8
→	Diameter	Height	Weight	Site	D2H			
10	4.09	5.73	0.78	1	95.852			
11	3.62	5.10	0.60	2	66.832			
12	4.77	5.54	1.11	2	126.051			
13	1.39	2.40	0.04	2	4.637			
14	2.89	4.48	0.32	2	37.417			
15	3.90	4.84	0.70	2	73.616			
16	1.52	2.90	0.07	2	6.700			

Step 5: Run the Regression Again

Now you are ready to run the regression again. Simply repeat the menu selection you made earlier. The Regression dialog box and Graphs subdialog box will contain the same settings as before. You are ready to go!

1 First, close all the graphs that you created before correcting the data. Choose **Window ➤ Close All Graphs** and click **OK**.

2 Choose **Stat ➤ Regression ➤ Regression** and click **OK**.

Tip | To set a dialog box back to its defaults, press F3.

As before, MINITAB displays the text output in the Session window, and displays each of the three graphs in its own Graph window. First, look at the Session window output.

Session window output

Regression Analysis

```
The regression equation is
Weight = 0.0200 + 0.00829 D2H

Predictor          Coef         StDev           T          P
Constant        0.01999       0.01365        1.46      0.160
D2H           0.0082897     0.0002390       34.68      0.000

S = 0.03880     R-Sq = 98.5%     R-Sq(adj) = 98.4%
Analysis of Variance

Source           DF          SS          MS          F          P
Regression        1      1.8108      1.8108    1202.89      0.000
Residual Error   18      0.0271      0.0015
Total            19      1.8379

Unusual Observations
Obs      D2H      Weight        Fit    StDev Fit    Residual    St Resid
 12      126     1.11000    1.06492      0.02142     0.04508        1.39 X
 17      107     0.79000    0.90858      0.01740    -0.11858       -3.42R

R denotes an observation with a large standardized residual
X denotes an observation whose X value gives it large influence.
```

If you have a good model and have satisfied all the statistical assumptions, then you can measure the diameter and height of any poplar in this population and be able to predict its weight without cutting it down, drying it, and weighing it on a scale.

From the regression output, you see a high t-ratio and a low p-value for D2H in the table of coefficients, indicating strong evidence of a relationship between D2H and Weight. The large F-statistic and low p-value in the analysis of variance table quantify this relationship in a different way. The R^2 and adjusted R^2 values of greater than 98% further reinforce the assertion that there is a strong linear relationship between D2H and Weight.

Before making a final conclusion, however, you decide to look at the plots.

Graph window output

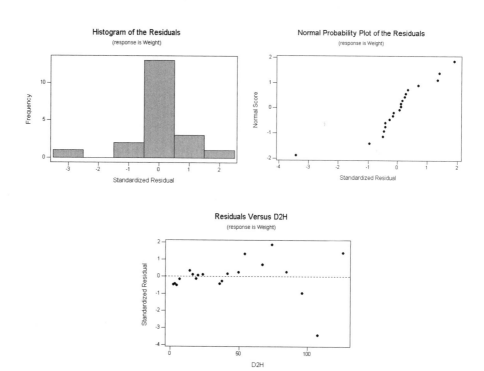

You notice from the Residuals versus D2H plot that the variance does not appear to be constant—an important assumption for a regression model to meet. It is larger at bigger values of D2H. In the interest of time we will continue with our session, but this is something you would want to examine more closely.

Step 6: Draw a Fitted Regression Line

Next, you want to display a scatter plot with the regression line drawn on it to see how closely the measured data lie to the least-squares regression line.

To plot Weight versus D2H:

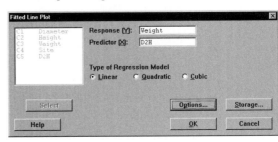

1 Choose **Stat ➤ Regression ➤ Fitted Line Plot**.

2 In **Response (Y)**, enter *Weight*.

3 In **Predictor (X)**, enter *D2H*. Click **OK**.

Graph window output

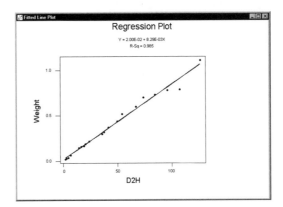

Step 7: Change the Graph Title

You would like to change the title of your graph. You could redo the dialog box and add a title in the Options subdialog box. You can also edit the graph directly, after it has been created.

MINITAB's Graph Editor is very similar to most drawing packages. If you know how to use a drawing package, you should be able to edit MINITAB graphs very easily.

In this step, you will learn how to:

- enter graph editing mode
- change the text of the title
- resize the text box so that the title fits on one line

Put the graph in edit mode

1 Make the Graph window active by clicking on it or choosing its name from the Window menu.

2 Maximize the Graph window.

3 Choose **Editor ➤ Edit**.

More | A graph can be in one of three modes: *View mode* allows you to view your graph but nothing else; *Edit mode* allows you to edit your graph; and *Brush mode* allows you to brush your graph (that is, identify points). Choose the mode from the Editor menu.

4 Two palettes should appear. If they do not, open them:

- Choose **Editor ➤ Show Tool Palette**.

- Choose **Editor ➤ Show Attribute Palette**.

Your Graph window should look like this:

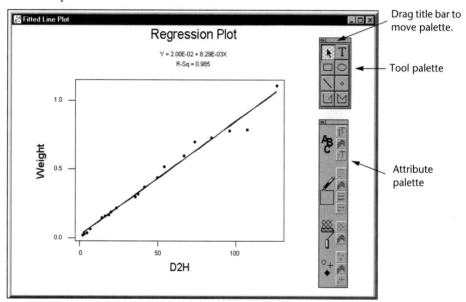

Your palettes may be in different positions. You can move a palette around the way you move a dialog box around—by dragging the title bar at the top of the palette.

Change the text of the title

1 On the Tool palette, click the selection tool if it is not already selected.

2 Click anywhere on the title and press (Enter), or double-click on the title.

A text box containing the current title will appear on the screen:

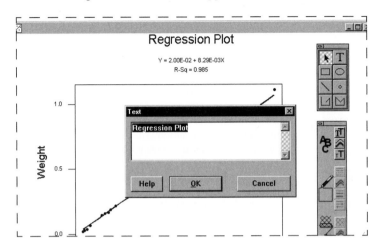

3 In the box, edit the title to say *Regression Plot for Poplar2 Data*. Click **OK**.

Resize the text box of the title

Because the title is longer, it is now on three lines. You need to resize the box that surrounds the title.

1 If necessary, click on the title to make it active. Handles will appear.

2 Place the cursor on the middle handle on the right edge. The cursor changes to crossed diagonal lines.

3 Click and hold the mouse button down and drag the right edge so the title is on two lines.

4 Place the cursor on the middle handle on the left edge. Click and hold the mouse button down and drag the left edge until the title is on one line.

Now you can position the title where you want it.

5 Put the cursor in the middle of the title.

6 Click and hold the mouse button down and drag the title to the position you want. Release the mouse button.

Step 8: Make the Regression Line Red

You decide to make the regression line red, so it is easier to see.

1 Click anywhere on the regression line. Handles will appear.

2 On the Attribute palette, click the line color tool ⬆ . A Color palette appears.

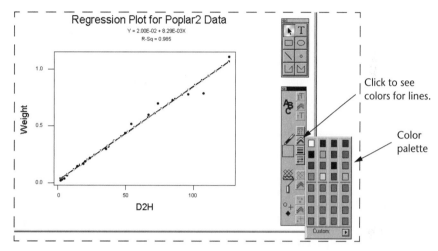

3 Click the red square. The line will become red.

4 Click in a blank space on the graph to remove the handles.

Step 9: Brush the Graph to Identify Points

One point has a very large value for D2H. You want to know what point this is. Brushing allows you to identify points on a plot. Switch to Brush mode, and open the Brushing palette if necessary.

1 Choose **Editor ➤ Brush**.

2 If the Brushing palette does not appear (see below), choose **Editor ➤ Show Brushing Palette**. Your cursor will change to a hand.

3 Click on the point you want to identify. Its row number appears in the Brushing palette.

Brushing
palette

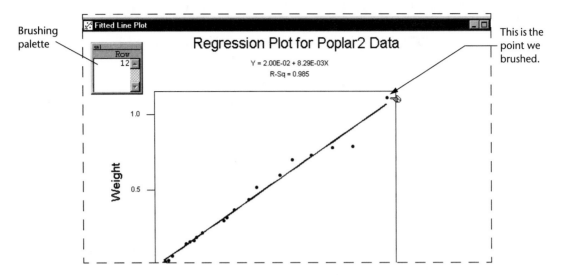

This is the
point we
brushed.

Suppose you would like more information on points you select. You can include data
for up to ten worksheet columns in the Brushing palette.

1   Choose **Editor ➤ Set ID Variables**.

2   Click **Use columns**, then enter *C1–C4*.

3   Click **OK**.

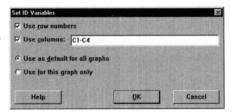

The Brushing palette widens to display the additional information. If you like, you can
move it so both the palette and the plot can be easily seen.

You want to identify the two points on the extreme right of the plot. You can select a
block of points by enclosing them in a rectangle. To draw the rectangle, you begin at
the upper-left corner and drag down to the lower-right corner of the rectangle.

4   Move the cursor to the location where you want to begin drawing the rectangle.
    This location will be the upper-left corner.

5   Hold the mouse button down and drag down to the lower-right until the rectangle
    encloses the two points.

The points are enclosed in a rectangle and identified in the Brushing palette.

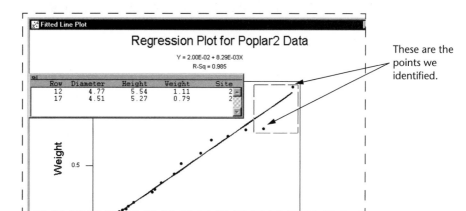

These are the points we identified.

These are the same points identified previously as being an outlier and influential observation. Here, brushing lets you quickly see the diameter, height, weight, and site information for these points.

The brushed points are also marked in the Data window.

brushed points

		C1	C2	C3	C4	C5	C6	C7	C8
	→	Diameter	Height	Weight	Site	D2H			
11		3.62	5.10	0.60	2	66.832			
12		4.77	5.54	1.11	2	126.051			
13		1.39	2.40	0.04	2	4.637			
14		2.89	4.48	0.32	2	37.417			
15		3.90	4.84	0.70	2	73.616			
16		1.52	2.90	0.07	2	6.700			
17		4.51	5.27	0.79	2	107.192			
18		1.18	2.20	0.03	2	3.063			
19		3.17	4.93	0.44	2	49.541			

Step 10: Save and Exit

1 Choose **File ➤ Save Project**.

2 In **File name**, enter *POPLAR2* for the name of your project. If you omit the extension .MPJ, MINITAB will automatically add it once you save the project.

3 Click **Save**.

4 If you see a message box asking if you want to replace an existing file, click **Yes**.

5 If you want to take a break at this point, you can exit MINITAB by choosing **File ➤ Exit**, or you can go on to Session Three.

10

Session Three: Advanced MINITAB

Chapter 10

Overview of Session Three

The story

How feasible are energy plantations? How much wood for energy can you realistically expect from these plantations, and how can you maximize yield?

In an effort to maximize yield, the researchers designed an experiment to determine how two factors, Site and Treatment, influence the weight of four-year-old poplar clones. They planted trees on two sites: Site 1—a moist site with rich soil, and Site 2—a dry, sandy site. They applied four different treatments to the trees: Treatment 1 was the control (no treatment), Treatment 2 was fertilizer, Treatment 3 was irrigation, and Treatment 4 was both fertilizer and irrigation. To account for a variety of weather conditions, the researchers replicated the data by planting half the trees in Year 1, and the other half in Year 2.

As data analyst for the project, you will perform the statistical analysis on the sample data stored in the MINITAB file called POPLAR4.MTW.

What you will learn

In this session, you will learn how to:

- quickly generate basic statistics to describe the variables you are interested in
- change the codes the field researchers were using for missing values into missing value codes that MINITAB will recognize
- subset the data to focus on just the group of trees that you want to examine further
- create boxplots to see at a glance the differences between categories of trees
- use analysis of variance to determine which variables are contributing to the differences between trees

Time required

About 25 minutes.

Step 1: Start a New Project

- If you are not already running MINITAB, start the program.

- If you have just completed Session Two, start a new project: choose **File ➤ New**, click **Minitab Project**, then click **OK**.

If you have not saved your changes to the previous project, MINITAB will give you the chance to do so.

Step 2: Open a Worksheet

You will get data from a MINITAB saved worksheet named POPLAR4.MTW that is located in the DATA subdirectory or folder.

1 Choose **File ➤ Open Worksheet**.

2 Move to the DATA subdirectory and select the file POPLAR4.MTW. Click **Open**.

Two windows can show you information about this worksheet.

3 Choose **Window ➤ Info** or press Ctrl+I.

The Info window displays summary information on your current worksheet; it updates automatically as your worksheet changes.

4 If the worksheet is not visible, open the Data window by pressing Ctrl+D.

The Data window shows you the columns of data in detail.

This worksheet contains seven variables: Site, Year, Treatment (experimental treatment), Diameter (cm), Height (m), Weight (kg), and Age (years).

	C1	C2	C3	C4	C5	C6	C7	C8
→	Site	Year	Treatment	Diameter	Height	Weight	Age	
1	1	1	1	2.23	3.76	0.17	3	
2	1	1	1	2.12	3.15	0.15	3	
3	1	1	1	1.06	1.85	0.02	3	
4	1	1	1	2.12	3.64	0.16	3	
5	1	1	1	2.99	4.64	0.37	3	
6	1	1	1	4.01	5.25	0.73	3	
7	1	1	1	2.41	4.07	0.22	3	

Tip | If you want to adjust the column widths to fit the data, point with your mouse to the top of a line dividing two columns until the mouse cursor turns into a two-sided arrow. Then, press the mouse button down and drag the column border to make it wider or narrower.

Step 3: Generate Descriptive Statistics

You want to maximize yield, so you will focus on what factors influence the weight of trees. Begin by looking at the descriptive statistics for the variable Weight.

1 Choose **Stat ➤ Basic Statistics ➤ Display Descriptive Statistics**.

2 In **Variables**, enter *Weight*. Click **OK**.

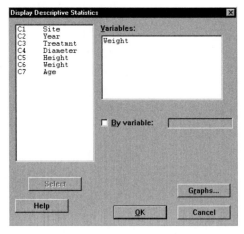

Session window output

Descriptive Statistics

Variable	N	Mean	Median	TrMean	StDev	SE Mean
Weight	291	1.057	1.630	1.974	10.370	0.608

Variable	Minimum	Maximum	Q1	Q3
Weight	-99.000	6.930	0.600	3.420

Notice the minimum value for Weight. It is certainly impossible to have a weight of −99 kilograms! The real story here is that our data gatherers in the field recorded the value −99 to represent a dead tree.

Leaving values of −99 in the worksheet is going to considerably throw off any analyses you do. In fact, it has already affected the output of the descriptive statistics just computed. The means and medians are artificially low, while the standard deviation is artificially high. You need to convert all −99's to missing values.

Missing values do not affect the results of any statistical analyses. MINITAB represents a missing value for numerical data with an asterisk (∗).

Step 4: Recode the Data

MINITAB provides many data manipulation tools. One of the most useful is the Code command, which allows you change all the occurrences of one value into another value. In this case, you want to change all the −99's to ∗, the missing value symbol.

1   Choose **Manip ➤ Code ➤ Numeric to Numeric**.

2   In **Code data from columns**, enter *Weight*.

3   In **Into columns**, enter *Weight*. This will replace the old values in Weight with the new, coded values.

4   In **Original values**, type −99. This is the value you want to change.

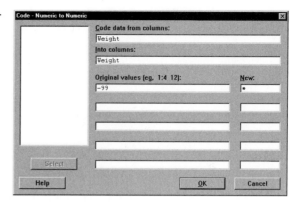

5   In **New**, type *. This is the missing value symbol. Click **OK**.

In the Data window, you will see that all occurrences of the value −99 in the variable Weight have been replaced with *, the code for a missing data value.

Step 5: Tally the Data

How many trees of each age are you dealing with? Use the Tally command to find out:

1   Choose **Stat ➤ Tables ➤ Tally**.

2   In **Variables**, enter *Age*. Click **OK**.

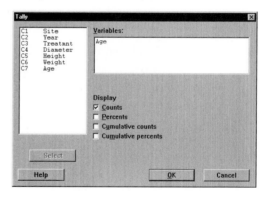

Session window output

Summary Statistics for Discrete Variables

Age	Count
3	144
4	147
N=	291

The output shows that you have 144 three-year-old trees, and 147 four-year-old trees.

Step 6: Split the Data by Age

Suppose you want to analyze the data for just the four-year-old trees. Here is a technique you can use to create a new data set with just the four-year-old trees.

Make a separate worksheet for the four-year-old trees

1 Choose **Manip ➤ Split Worksheet**.

2 In **By variables**, enter *Age*. Click **OK**.

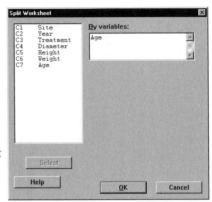

MINITAB will split the POPLAR4 worksheet using the values of Age. Since there are two unique values in the age column (3 and 4), MINITAB will create two new worksheets. The worksheet that contains the data for the three-year-old trees will be named POPLAR4.MTW(Age = 3); the worksheet that contains the data for the four-year-old trees will be named POPLAR4.MTW(Age = 4).

Rename the worksheet that contains the four-year-old trees' data

1 Choose **Window ➤ Manage Worksheets**.

2 Click on **POPLAR4.MTW(Age = 4)**.

3 Click **Rename**.

4 Type *4YROLDS.MTW*.

5 Click **OK** and then click **Done**.

You will now perform the analysis on the four-year-old poplar data.

Step 7: Check for Normality with a Histogram

You will now create a histogram of the variable Weight.

1 Make sure the Data window named 4YROLDS.MTW is active. To make a Data window active, click on it, or choose its name from the Window menu. Notice that the active Data window has asterisks after its name.

2 Choose **Graph ➤ Histogram**.

3 In **X**, enter *Weight*. Click **OK**.

After a few seconds, the histogram appears in its own window.

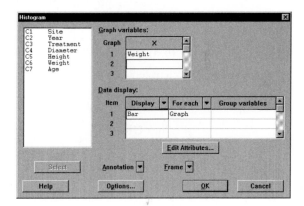

Graph window output

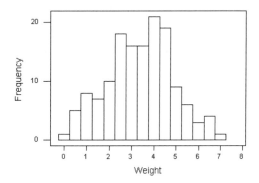

The weights of the poplars are approximately normally distributed (in a bell-shaped curve).

Step 8: Compare Weight by Treatment with Boxplots

Now you will want to look at the weight for each treatment. Boxplots are good for graphically comparing different levels of a variable.

1 Choose **Graph ➤ Boxplot**.

2 In **Y**, enter *Weight*.

3 In **X**, enter *Treatment*.

This tells MINITAB to produce a separate boxplot of weight for each treatment.

4 Click **OK**.

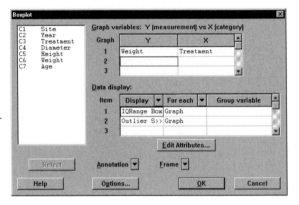

Graph window output

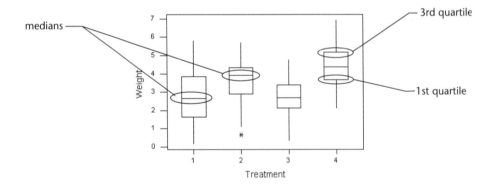

The line drawn across each box indicates the median, or middle, of the data. The bottom and top edges of the box mark the first (25th percentile) and third (75th percentile) quartiles, respectively.

The boxplots suggest that Treatments 2 and 4 (fertilizer and fertilizer/irrigation) have produced the heaviest trees, while Treatments 1 and 3 (control and irrigation) have yielded lighter trees.

You might also expect the site to have an impact on weight. The Site 1 trees planted in the rich, well-drained soil would be expected to weigh more than the Site 2 trees planted in the dry, sandy soil. You can determine if this assumption is true by looking at a boxplot of weight for each site.

Rather than repeat your previous menu selection from the beginning, recall the last Boxplot dialog box and change the X, or category, variable.

5 Choose **Edit ➤ Edit Last Dialog**, or press Ctrl+E.

6 In X, enter *Site*.

7 Click **OK**.

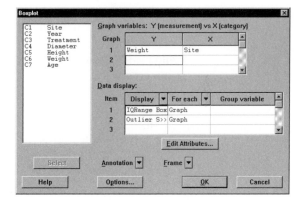

Graph window output

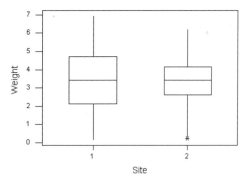

Surprisingly, the Site 1 tree weights do not seem very different from the Site 2 tree weights. The spreads are different for each site, but the medians are almost the same.

Step 9: Perform an Analysis of Variance

You have seen from the boxplots that poplar weights differ noticeably among the four treatments, but not as noticeably between the two sites. Now you decide to use analysis of variance to see if there are statistically significant differences in weight due to the different levels of the factors site and treatment.

1 Choose **Stat ➤ ANOVA ➤ Balanced ANOVA**.

2 In **Responses**, enter *Weight*.

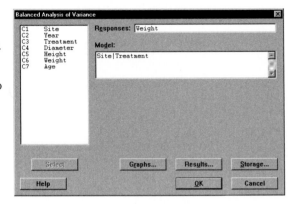

Next, you will enter the model you want MINITAB to fit. You decide to look at a model with site, treatment, and the site*treatment interaction.

3 In **Model**, type *Site | Treatment*.

The vertical bar tells MINITAB that you want to include all possible interactions in the model. To make a vertical bar on most keyboards, press (Shift)+(\), or you can use the symbol ! instead.

4 Click **OK**.

Session window output

Analysis of Variance (Balanced Designs)

```
Factor      Type Levels Values

Site        fixed    2    1    2
Treatmen    fixed    4    1    2    3    4
```

Analysis of Variance for Weight

Source	DF	SS	MS	F	P
Site	1	1.022	1.022	0.63	0.429
Treatmen	3	79.807	26.602	16.36	0.000
Site*Treatmen	3	7.652	2.551	1.57	0.200
Error	136	221.203	1.626		
Total	143	309.683			

Balanced ANOVA lists each factor in the model and the number of levels in each factor. Next it lists the analysis of variance table, which provides F-values, p-values, and other information on each of the specified variables and their interaction.

Suppose you want to perform an F-test for each effect in the model. For example, to test the null hypothesis that the treatment effect is the same for both sites (the Site * Treatment interaction), compare MINITAB's p-value with the commonly used level of .05. Because the p-value is 0.200 (a value larger than .05) you cannot reject the null hypothesis. That is, you cannot conclude that the treatment effect differs for the two sites.

Now you can look at the main effects, Site and Treatment. The Site p-value of 0.429 is also larger than .05, so you cannot conclude that poplar weights differ significantly between the 2 sites. The p-value for Treatment is small (0.000) thereby supporting the conclusion that mean weights do differ significantly for different treatments.

This agrees with what you saw earlier in the boxplots—that poplar weights were different for different treatments, but only varied slightly between the two sites. Before you decide that Treatment is the only important factor influencing poplar weight, take a look at the Year effect—remember that the researchers planted half the trees in Year 1 and half in Year 2.

Step 10: Compare Weight by Year with Boxplots

You decide to look at a boxplot to compare the weight of poplars planted in Year 1 with those planted in Year 2.

1   Choose **Graph ➤ Boxplot**.

2   In **Y**, enter *Weight*.

3   In **X**, enter *Year*.

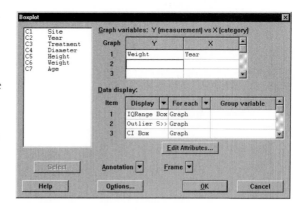

This says to draw a separate boxplot of weight for each year.

Notice the first two rows of the **Data display** table. **IQRange Box** instructs MINITAB to display a box showing the interquartile range, from the 25th to the 75th percentile. **Outlier Symbol** instructs MINITAB to display an asterisk (∗) for all outlier values. You decide to also display a confidence interval box within the IQ Range Box.

4   In the **Data display** table, in the **Display** column, click in the row for item 3.

5   Click the down arrow beside **Display**, and choose **CI Box**.

6   Click in the next cell to the right.

7   Click the down arrow beside **For each** and choose **Graph**.

This row tells MINITAB to include a confidence interval on each boxplot.

By default, MINITAB draws boxplots vertically, but you also can draw them horizontally.

8   Click **Options**.

9   Check **Transpose X and Y**, then click **OK** twice.

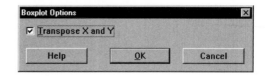

*Graph
window
output*

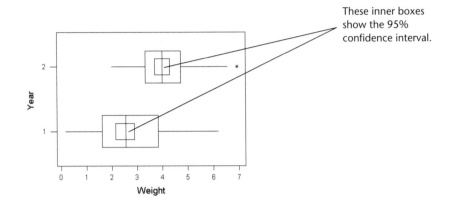

These inner boxes
show the 95%
confidence interval.

The inner boxes show a 95% confidence interval for the median. The boxplot suggests that poplars planted in Year 2 are heavier than those planted in Year 1. But why is year important? Trees were planted in two different years simply to replicate the data.

You interview the field researchers and learn that they did not apply herbicides to control weeds during the first year planting. As a result, many young trees either died or were severely stunted. To improve the trees' ability to survive, researchers did apply herbicides when they planted poplars the second year.

You draw three preliminary conclusions from your analysis. One, fertilization appears to be an effective way to maximize the weight of poplar clones. Two, it is important to control weeds while the trees are very young. Three, given proper planting and nutrient conditions, poplar clones may not require a high-quality site in order to yield a substantial amount of biomass.

Not only were the Year 2 trees heavier, their weights were more consistent. But before you recommend the use of herbicides and fertilizers, you want to look more closely at the Year 2 trees.

Specifically, you want to know if you still see Site and Treatment effects, when you look at the Year 2 trees alone.

Step 11: Quickly Repeat the Entire Analysis

You decide to repeat the analysis on Year 2 trees only. First, you need to create this subset by splitting the data you just used for the four-year-old trees. Then, rather than redoing all the dialog boxes to repeat the analysis, you will use MINITAB's History window and the Command Line Editor.

Split the POPLAR4 worksheet using the values of Year

1 Make sure the Data window named POPLAR4.MTW is active. To make a Data window active, click on it, or choose its name from the Window menu.

2 Choose **Manip ➤ Split Worksheet**.

3 In **By variables**, enter *Year*. Click **OK**.

Rename the worksheet that contains the data for the Year 2 trees

1 Choose **Window ➤ Manage Worksheets**.

2 Click the new worksheet: **POPLAR4.MTW(Year = 2)**.

3 Click **Rename**.

4 Type *YEAR2.MTW*.

5 Click **OK** and then click **Done**.

Repeat the analysis on the Year 2 trees

1 Make sure the Data window named YEAR2.MTW is active. To make a Data window active, click on it, or choose its name from the Window menu.

2 Open the History window by choosing **Window ➤ History** or pressing Ctrl+H.

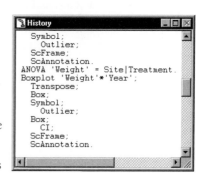

3 Scroll back in the History window until you find the command "Histogram."

This was the command you used to check for normality.

4 Select everything from "Histogram" to the line above "Split."

5 Choose **Edit ➤ Command Line Editor**, or as a shortcut, press Ctrl+L.

A dialog box containing the MINITAB commands from the section you highlighted appears.

This dialog box is a simple editor. You can scroll, delete text, type text, and highlight a block of text.

Cut, copy, and paste text using the keyboard: cut with Ctrl +X, copy with Ctrl +C, and paste with Ctrl +V.

6 Click **Submit Commands**.

The entire analysis, a histogram of Weight, boxplots of Weight by Treatment and Weight by Site, an analysis of variance, and a boxplot of Weight by Year are all done, with no further work.

Step 12: Save and Exit

1 Choose **File ➤ Save Project**.

2 In **File name**, enter *POPLAR4* for the name of your project. If you omit the extension .MPJ, MINITAB will automatically add it once you save the project.

3 Click **Save**.

4 If you see a message box asking if you want to replace an existing file, click **Yes**.

5 If you want to take a break at this point, you can exit MINITAB by choosing **File ➤ Exit**, or you can go on to Session Four.

11

Session Four: Quality Control and Improvement

Overview of Session Four

The story

You work for an automobile manufacturer in a department that assembles engines. One of the parts, a camshaft, must be 600 mm ±2 mm long to meet engineering specifications. There has been a chronic problem with camshaft length being out of specification — a problem which has caused poor-fitting assemblies down the production line and high scrap and rework rates.

Your supervisor wants to run $\overline{X}$ and R charts to monitor this characteristic. For a month, data are collected on the length of five camshafts per shift (1 sample of size 5 per shift). You have been asked to lead a problem-solving team and recommend a solution.

What you will learn

In this session you will learn how to:

- produce $\overline{X}$ and R charts

- produce histograms with normal curves

- perform process capability analysis

Time required

About 20 minutes.

Step 1: Start a New Project

- If you are not already running MINITAB, start the program.

- If you have just completed Session Three, start a new project: choose **File ➤ New**, click **Minitab Project**, then click **OK**.

If you have not saved your changes to the previous project, MINITAB will give you the chance to do so.

Step 2: Open a Worksheet

You will get data from a MINITAB saved worksheet named CAMSHAFT.MTW that is located in the DATA subdirectory or folder.

1   Choose **File ➤ Open Worksheet**.

2   Move to the DATA subdirectory and select the file CAMSHAFT.MTW. Click **Open**.

3   If it is not visible, open the Data window by pressing Ctrl+D.

The Data window shows you the columns of data in detail.

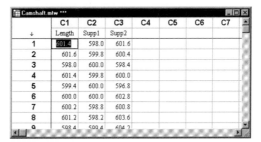

This worksheet contains the results of the sampling plan from the last month. For now, you are concerned with the first column, Length, which contains 100 observations (20 samples of 5 camshafts each). Recall that the camshaft lengths are measured in millimeters.

Step 3: Examine Ranges with an R Chart

First, you want to produce a control chart to look at the range of camshaft lengths within the sample subgroups. You hope the subgroup data do not range too far from the center line (the estimated average range), thus showing large variability.

1   Choose **Stat ➤ Control Charts ➤ R**.

2   In **Single column**, enter *Length*.

3   In **Subgroup size**, type *5*.

4   Click **OK**.

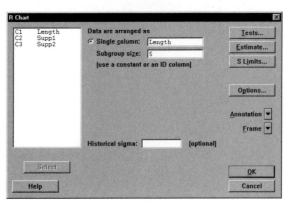

Graph window output

Each point represents a subgroup range (the highest value minus the lowest value in the subgroup).

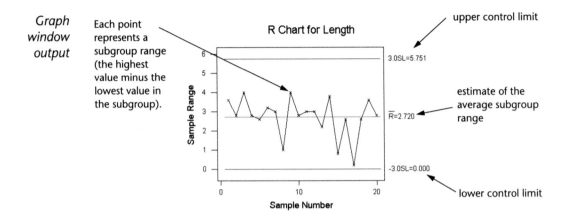

upper control limit

estimate of the average subgroup range

lower control limit

The R chart for Length does not show any points out of control, but you notice that the center line at 2.72 mm is quite large given that the maximum allowable variation is ±2 mm. There may be excess variability in our process.

Step 4: Test for Special Causes with an Xbar Chart

You will create an $\overline{X}$ chart to see if there is a problem with camshaft lengths being outside acceptable limits. In addition, you will instruct MINITAB to use eight common runs rules that point out special causes for variation.

1 Choose **Stat ► Control Charts ► Xbar**.

2 In **Single column**, enter *Length*.

3 In **Subgroup size**, type *5*.

4 Click **Tests**.

The Tests subdialog box appears.

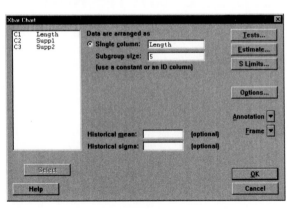

5 Choose **Perform all eight tests**.

6 Click **OK** twice.

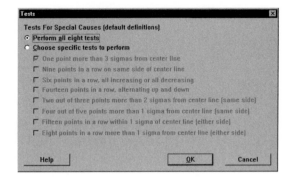

Graph window output

Each point represents a subgroup mean.

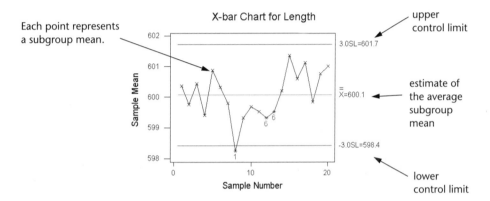

upper control limit

estimate of the average subgroup mean

lower control limit

The $\overline{X}$ chart shows that the process is out of control. Specifically, one point has failed test 1, and two points have failed test 6. To find out what these tests mean, look in the Session window.

7 Choose **Window ▶ Session**.

Session window output

```
TEST 1. One point more than 3.00 sigmas from center line.
Test Failed at points: 8

TEST 6. 4 out of 5 points more than 1 sigma from center line
        (on one side of CL).
Test Failed at points: 12 13
```

The process produced one point more than 3 sigmas from the center line, and four of five points more than 1 sigma from the center line (on one side of the center line).

Now that you have confirmed that a problem does exist, it is time to look for causes and solutions. Unfortunately, the sampling plan did not allow for detailed inspection of precisely where and when the problems occurred because only one sample was taken per shift. A better plan would have been to take multiple samples per shift for the troubleshooting phase, and to switch to this monitoring plan after special causes were found and eliminated. Nonetheless, you are determined to get what you can out of the data that you have.

Step 5: Create a Histogram with Normal Curve

The histogram with normal curve is useful for examining a variable's distribution. You decide to examine the variable Length.

1   Choose **Stat ➤ Basic Statistics ➤ Display Descriptive Statistics**.

2   In **Variables**, enter *Length*.

3   Click **Graphs**.

    The Graphs subdialog box appears.

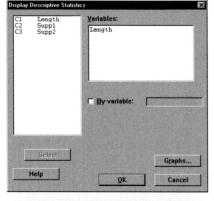

4   Check **Histogram of data, with normal curve**.

5   Click **OK** twice.

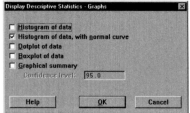

Graph window output

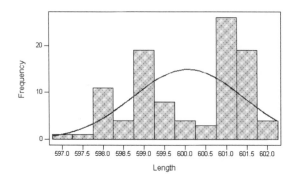

Histogram of Length, with Normal Curve

In general, we expect a variable such as Length to follow the normal distribution. In this case, the histogram would be approximately bell-shaped. The histogram you just created is certainly not bell-shaped. In fact, it would appear from the spikes at 598, 599, and 601 that we may be dealing with two separate and distinct distributions.

An examination of the inventory records indicates that there are two suppliers for the camshafts. Now you are starting to understand the odd histogram. You decide to obtain measurements from both suppliers and run $\overline{X}$ and R charts separately on each set of data with a subgroup size of 5 for each. The data for each supplier are stored in the columns Supp1 and Supp2 of your worksheet.

Step 6: Display Combined Xbar and R Charts

Your worksheet contains variables named Supp1 and Supp2 with data for Suppliers 1 and 2. You could repeat the same procedures to produce control charts for Supplier 1 as you did to produce the charts for Length. However, there is another command, Xbar-R, that you can use to display both charts together.

1 Choose **Stat ➤ Control Charts ➤ Xbar-R**.

2 In **Single column**, enter *Supp1*.

3 In **Subgroup size**, type *5*. Click **OK**.

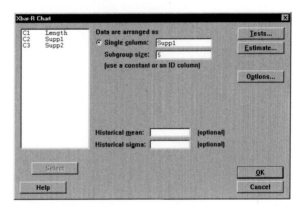

Graph window output

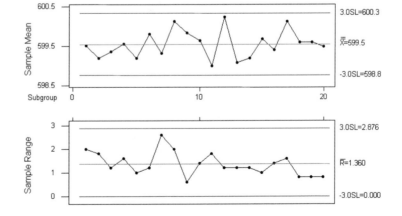

Xbar/R Chart for Supp1

Both the means and ranges for Supplier 1 appear to be in control, although you notice that the mean is 599.5 mm, not 600. The average range for Supplier 1 is 1.341 mm.

Evaluate Supplier 2

You can produce the same control charts for Supplier 2, using the variable named Supp2, as you did for Supplier 1.

1 Press Ctrl+E.

This keyboard shortcut, short for **Edit ➤ Edit Last Dialog**, brings up the Xbar-R Chart dialog box again.

2 In **Single column**, enter *Supp2*. Click **OK**.

You do not need to enter a subgroup size because it was still set to 5 from the last time you used this dialog box. MINITAB "remembers" the dialog box settings from the last time a dialog box was used in a session.

Graph window output

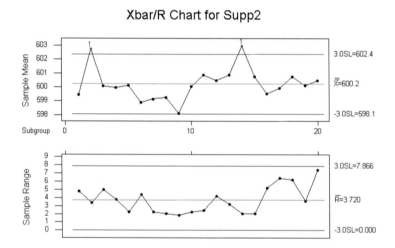

Xbar/R Chart for Supp2

Supplier 2's $\overline{X}$ chart reveals problems. From the chart, you can see that two points are above the upper control limit.

The R chart does not indicate that the process is out of control. However, you notice that the center line is at 3.720, which is almost three times larger than Supplier 1's $\overline{R}$ of 1.341.

As team leader, you recommend that longer production runs be accepted from Supplier 1 until Supplier 2 can demonstrate that camshaft production is in control. You will work with Supplier 2 to reduce process variability to an acceptable level. Because of the statistical evidence to support your position, your recommendation is implemented.

Step 7: Save and Exit

1 Choose **File ➤ Save Project**.

2 In **File name**, enter *CAMSHFT1* for the name of your project. If you omit the extension .MPJ, MINITAB will automatically add it once you save the project.

3 Click **Save**.

4 If you see a message box asking if you want to replace an existing file, click **Yes**.

5 To close MINITAB choose **File ➤ Exit**.

INDEX

A

active cells 2-3
active Data window 1-5
adding comments in the Session window 6-4
adding titles to graphs 5-9
analysis of variance 4-2, 4-9
analyzing your data 4-1
    examples of 8-1, 9-1, 10-1, 11-1
arithmetic
    see Calculator
Attribute palette 1-4, 5-8, 9-9
attributes of data display elements 5-4

B

basic statistics 4-2
bitmap (BMP) file 5-11
BMP (bitmap) file 5-11
boxplots 4-10, 8-6, 10-8, 10-11
brushing graphs 5-10, 9-11
Brushing palette 5-10, 9-11

C

calculations
    see Calculator
Calculator 3-1, 3-12, 8-8
capabilities summary for Student 12
    x
cells
    active 2-3
    clearing 3-3
    copying 3-3
    cutting 3-3

deleting 3-3
    erasing 3-3
    inserting 3-4
    pasting 3-3
    restoring 2-6
character graphs 5-2
chi-square test 4-11
clearing cells 3-3
closing
    graphs 1-11
    projects 1-8
    worksheets 1-11
coding data 3-11, 10-4
columns 2-2
    based on a calculation 3-12
    combining 3-10
    compressing display of 3-5
    data types 3-5
    date/time 2-3
    descriptions of 3-5, 3-7
    displaying and hiding empty 3-5
    fixed number of decimals 3-6
    format 3-5
    hiding empty 3-5
    inserting 3-4
    moving 3-4
    name row of 2-3
    naming 3-4
    number row of 2-3
    sizing widths of 3-4, 3-5
    stacking 3-10
    text 2-3
combining columns 3-10
Command Line Editor 1-7, 7-2, 10-12
commands
    issuing 1-5
    menu 1-5
    output of 6-2
    session 1-7, 7-1
comments
    adding to output 8-11
    in column descriptions 3-7

in project descriptions 1-8
    in worksheet descriptions 2-10
compressing column display 3-5
confidence intervals 4-4
constants 2-2
    naming 2-3
control charts 4-2
    R charts 11-3
    Xbar charts 11-4
    Xbar-R charts 11-7
converting values 3-11
copying
    and pasting data 2-7
    blocks of Session window text 6-4
    cells 3-3
    graphs 5-11
    Session window output to the Data window 6-5
core graphs, creating 5-3
correcting data 2-6
correlation 4-5, 8-10
cross tabulation 4-11
cutting cells 3-3

D

data 2-1
    analyzing 4-1
    copying 2-7
    date/time 2-2, 3-6
    editing 2-6, 9-5
    entering patterned 8-4
    files, opening from 2-9
    numeric 2-2, 3-6
    opening from a file 2-9
    overview 2-2
    pasting 2-7
    patterned, entering 2-8
    recoding 3-11, 10-4
    saving 8-5
    splitting 3-7

I

identifier codes 3-10
identifying graph points 9-11
Info window 1-3, 2-4
inserting
    blank lines in the Session
        window 6-4
    cells 3-4
    columns 3-4
    rows 3-4
Internet, Minitab on the viii, 1-14
introduction to MINITAB 1-1
issuing commands 1-5

J

JPEG (Joint Photographic Experts
    Group, or JPG) file 5-11

L

least squares regression 4-7
list of features x
    Help file 1-13
Lotus 1-2-3 2-9

M

macros 7-4
managing Graph windows 5-7
manipulating data 3-1
marginal plots 5-7
mathematical functions
    see Calculator
means 4-3, 8-6, 10-4
medians 4-3, 8-6, 10-4
menu bar 1-4, 1-5
menu commands 1-5
    in the menu bar 1-5
    in the shortcut menus 1-5

merging files 2-10
MGF (MINITAB Graphics Format)
    files 5-11
Microsoft Windows (95, NT 4.0,
    NT 3.51)
    starting 1-2, 8-3
    using 1-2
MINITAB
    exiting 1-3
    starting 1-2
    stopping 1-2
MINITAB Graphics Format (MGF)
    files 5-11
MINITAB Portable Worksheet
    (MTP) files 2-9
MINITAB Project (MPJ) files 1-8,
    2-9
MINITAB Worksheet (MTW) files
    2-9
move to command output 6-2
moving columns 3-4
MPJ (MINITAB Project) files 1-8,
    2-9
MTB(MINITAB Exec) file 7-5
MTP (MINITAB Portable
    Worksheet) files 2-9
MTW (MINITAB Worksheet) files
    2-9

N

naming
    columns 3-4
    constants 2-3
    worksheets 10-6, 10-13
navigating in the Session window
    6-2
new
    projects 9-2
    worksheets 2-5
next command in the Session
    window 6-2
normal probability plot 4-10
numeric data 2-2, 3-6

O

object linking and embedding
    see OLE
OLE 5-11, 5-12
one-sample confidence interval 4-4
one-sample t-test 4-4
one-way analysis of variance 4-9
opening
    graphs 1-10, 5-11
    MINITAB program 8-3
    projects 1-8
    worksheets 1-10, 2-5, 2-9,
        2-10, 8-3
operating system, using your 1-2
overview of MINITAB 1-1

P

paired t-test 4-4
pasting
    cells 3-3
    data 2-7
    graphs 5-11
patterned data 2-8, 8-4
Pearson correlation coefficient 4-5,
    8-10
plots 5-3, 8-9
    fitted regression line 9-8
    residuals 9-7
preferences, saving 1-9
preview
    of a non-MINITAB file 2-10
    of a project file 2-10
    of a worksheet 2-10
previous command in the Session
    window 6-2
printing 8-11
    Data window 1-13
    files 2-9
    graphs 5-11
    Session window output 6-6,
        8-10
    windows 1-13, 8-11
probability distributions 3-13

U

undo a change in the Data window 2-6

unstacking columns 3-11

V

variable list box 1-6

variables, entering in a dialog box 1-6

W

web site viii, 1-14

window
    Data 1-3, 1-5, 2-3
    Graph 1-3, 5-7
    History 1-3, 7-3
    Info 1-3, 2-4
    Session 1-3, 2-4, 6-1

Windows (operating system)
    see Microsoft Windows

work flow in MINITAB 1-4

worksheet 1-5, 1-9, 2-2
    current 1-5
    description 2-10
    new 2-5
    opening 1-10, 2-10, 8-3
    previewing 2-10
    renaming 10-6, 10-13
    saving 2-9
    splitting 3-9, 10-6, 10-13

WWW address viii, 1-14

X

Xbar charts 4-13, 11-4

Xbar-R charts 4-13, 11-7

Z

Z-test 4-4